ANNE FRANK

Her life in words and pictures

from the archives of **THE ANNE FRANK HOUSE**

First Published 2004 in the Netherlands by the Anne Frank House under the title *The Story of Anne Frank*.
This American edition published under license from the Anne Frank House.

Anne Frank texts copyright © Anne Frank Fonds, Basel
Anne Frank family photographs © Anne Frank Stichting, Amsterdam/Anne Frank Fonds, Basel
This book © Anne Frank Stichting, Amsterdam, 2004

Flash Point is an imprint of Roaring Brook Press, a division of Holtzbrinck Publishing Holdings Limited Partnership.
175 Fifth Avenue, New York, New York 10010
Jacket and cover design by Edward Miller
Cataloging-in-Publication data is on file at the Library of Congress

Hardcover ISBN: 978-1-59643-546-9 / Paperback ISBN: 978-1-59643-547-6

Roaring Brook Press books are available for special promotions and premiums.
For details contact: Director of Special Markets, Holtzbrinck Publishers.

First American Edition September 2009
Printed in January 2010 in China by C&C Joint Printing Co., Ltd., Shenzhen, Guangdong Province
3 5 7 9 10 8 6 4

ANNE FRANK
Her life in words and pictures
from the archives of THE ANNE FRANK HOUSE

Menno Metselaar and Ruud van der Rol

Translated by Arnold J. Pomerans

Rb
Flash
Point

Roaring Brook Press

New York

Contents

One of my nicest presents

→

Anne was given this diary
on her thirteenth birthday.

smoeige foto hè !!!!

Ik zal hoop ik aan jou alles kunnen
toevertrouwen, zoals ik het nog aan
niemand gekund heb, en ik hoop dat
je een grote steun voor me zult zijn.

Anne Frank. 12 Juni 1942.

Ik heb tot nu een grote steun aan je gehad,
en ook aan onze lieve club die ik nu geregeld
schrijf, deze manier om in mijn dagboek te
schrijven vind ik veel
prettiger, en nu kan
ik het wu haast
niet afwachten als
ik tijd heb om in je te
schrijven. 28 Sept. 1942.
Anne Frank.

Annelies Marië Frank

1941/
1942. (winter)

Ik ben, o, zo blij dat ik je meegenomen heb.

On June 12, 1942, Anne Frank woke at six o'clock. It was her thirteenth birthday and she could hardly wait to get up. She hadn't been able to celebrate her previous two birthdays properly. On her eleventh birthday, the Germans had just occupied the Netherlands and no one had felt like having a party. When she was twelve, her grandmother was so ill that her birthday was missed then as well.

Anne managed to wait until a quarter to seven. Then she got up and went to the dining room of their house in Merwedeplein, Amsterdam. Moortje, the cat, welcomed her by meowing and rubbing against her legs. At seven o'clock Anne woke her father and mother. When the whole family was sitting around the breakfast table, she was finally allowed to open her presents: a game, candy, a gift token for two books, a puzzle, a brooch, and a diary.

←

Anne pasted a photograph of herself onto the first page of her diary, with the comment, **Gorgeous photograph, isn't it!!!!**

→

Anne started her diary with the following sentence: **I hope I will be able to confide everything to you, as I have never been able to confide in anyone, and I hope you will be a great source of comfort and support.** (June 12, 1942)

The diary was one of Anne's nicest presents. She had been able to choose it herself in the local bookshop. Anne intended to put everything she thought important in the diary, especially things she could not discuss with her friends. Anne filled her diary with letters she wrote to an imagined girlfriend, whom she called "Kitty."

Anne began her diary right away, on her birthday. First she said a few things about her classmates at school. After that she introduced herself and told her new "girlfriend" what her life had been like, at length.

Ik zal hoop ik aan jou alles kunnen toevertrouwen, zoals ik het nog aan niemand gekund heb, en ik hoop dat je een grote steun van me zult zijn. Anne Frank. 12 Juni 1942.

1925-1933

A German girl

My father, the most adorable father I have ever seen, didn't marry my mother until he was thirty-six and she was twenty-five. My sister, Margot, was born in Frankfurt am Main in Germany in 1926. I was born on June 12, 1929.

(from Anne's diary, June 20, 1942)

Anne Frank was born in 1929 in Frankfurt am Main in Germany. Her sister, Margot, was three years old at the time. Otto Frank worked in his family's bank. Anne's mother, Edith Frank Holländer, stayed home with the girls. The family was Jewish. They went to synagogue now and then and observed the most important Jewish holidays.

At the time, Germany was suffering. An economic crisis brought poverty and unemployment. A politician named Adolf Hitler* claimed that he could solve the crisis. Adolf Hitler and his party, the NSDAP,* were anti-Semitic.* They hated Jews and blamed them for all Germany's problems.

In 1932 Hitler won elections and in 1933 he and his Nazi party seized power. His government abolished democracy, forming a dictatorship.* Political opponents were arrested. Like so many other German Jews, Otto and Edith Frank were very worried about the future.

* Terms followed by an asterisk are explained in the Glossary, pp. 210–215.

←
Wedding photograph of Otto Frank and Edith Holländer. They were married on May 12, 1925, Otto Frank's birthday.

On February 16, 1926, Otto and Edith Frank had their first child, a girl whom they named Margot. Otto Frank took many snapshots of his children. The photographs on the next few pages all come from the Frank family photograph albums.

←
Baby Margot in the bath.

Margot as a toddler in her new
rainwear. She was staying with her
grandmother in Aachen.

Margot with two friends playing in the garden, June 1929.

→

Anne Frank was born on June 12, 1929. Her father took this photograph in the hospital one day later.

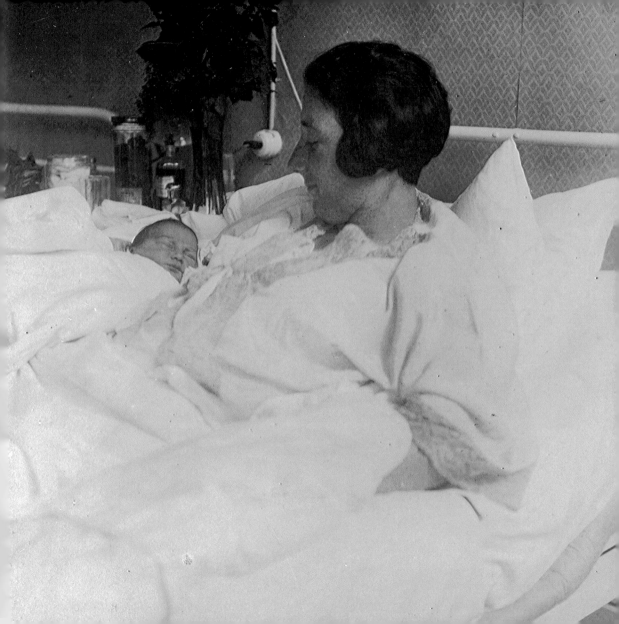

Margot is allowed to hold her little sister.

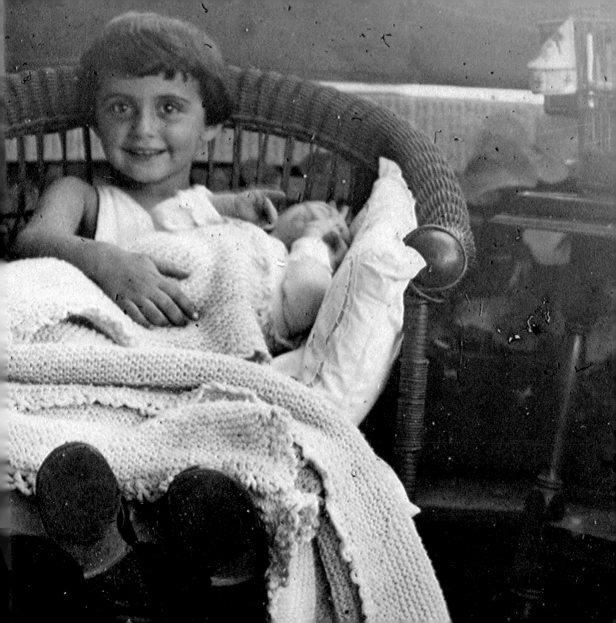

Margot (center) visiting Grammy Frank in
Frankfurt, together with her cousins Buddy
(right) and Stephan (left). The children
adored this grandmother, who told them
lovely stories all the time.

Margot (left) playing with
children from the neigh-
borhood on a hot day in
July.

→

Anne, May 1930

Margot regularly used the
sun lamp in the winter. The
goggles protected her eyes
from the fierce artificial
light.

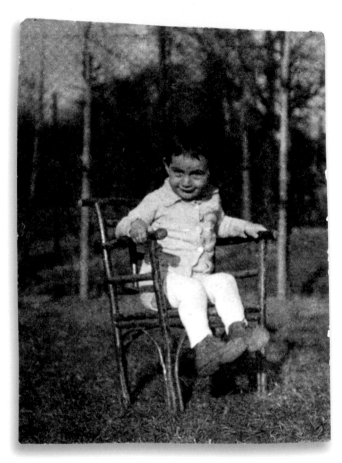

Anne at almost
two years old

Anne's mother giving her a taste of something. Margot and her cousin Stephan are looking on.

Otto Frank with Margot
and Anne, August 1931

Margot, December 1931

Margot and Anne on a hot
summer's day in 1932. Their
neighbor Grace is giving them
a shower.

Margot doing some knitting
and Anne making a project,
Christmas 1932.

1933

Leaving Germany

I lived in Frankfurt until I was four. Because we're Jewish, my father emigrated to Holland in 1933, where he became the Managing Director of the Dutch Opekta Company, which manufactures products used in making jam. My mother, Edith Holländer Frank, went with him to Holland in September, while Margot and I were sent to Aachen to stay with our grandmother. Margot went to Holland in December, and I followed in February, when I was plonked down on the table as a birthday present for Margot.

(June 20, 1942)

Otto and Edith Frank's fears about their future in Germany were proved right. In April 1933 the Hitler government took a variety of anti-Semitic measures. Jews were discriminated* against. Jewish teachers and civil servants were dismissed. At school, Jewish children were bullied and called names. Otto and Edith Frank decided to leave Germany. They were not the only ones. Thousands of people, Hitler's political opponents, artists, and scientists, including many Jews, fled Germany.

In the summer of 1933, Otto Frank left for Amsterdam. With the help of Erich Elias, his brother-in-law, he founded a company in Amsterdam manufacturing products used in jam-making. The company was called Opekta. Otto and Edith Frank left their rented house in Frankfurt, and Margot, Anne, and their mother were sent to stay with Grandma Holländer. She lived close to the Dutch border in Aachen, Germany. Edith Frank went over to Amsterdam from time to time, looking for a place to live. In November she found an apartment in one of a group of recently built houses in Merwedeplein. In December 1933, when she had furnished the apartment, she brought Margot over. Anne followed two months later. In the Netherlands Otto and Edith Frank felt safe and free. There was no Nazi government to make their life a torment.

$\rightarrow$

On March 10, 1933, the Frank family went out shopping in Frankfurt. Hitler had by then been in power for six weeks. Two days later, the Nazis won the Frankfurt municipal elections.

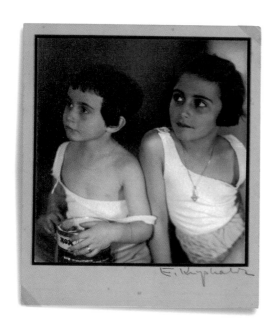

These photographs of Anne and Margot Frank were taken by a local photographer in Aachen in October 1933. They and their mother were staying with their grandmother. By then, Otto Frank had already been living in Amsterdam for a few months. He was hard at work getting his new company off the ground.

1934-1939

At home in the Netherlands

I started right away at the Montessori nursery school. I stayed there until I was six, at which time I started in the first form.... Our lives were not without anxiety, since our relatives in Germany were suffering under Hitler's anti-Jewish laws. After the pogroms in 1938 my two uncles (my mother's brothers) fled Germany, finding safe refuge in North America. My elderly grandmother came to live with us. She was seventy-three years old at the time.

(June 20, 1942)

Otto Frank had to work hard and was not at home very often. Anne's mother was all alone during the day and at first she felt homesick for Germany. But they simply could not go back. Germany had become a very dangerous place for Jews. There were banners and signs in many towns and villages with the words "Jews not wanted here." Special laws that discriminated even further against Jews had been passed forbidding them, for instance, from marrying non-Jews.

Hitler and his government were preparing for war. Special roads were being constructed, and tanks, airplanes, and guns were being produced. The unemployed were put to work on large construction projects and in the arms industry. As a result, the German economy picked up and Hitler gained more and more fanatical supporters. After a while, the Frank family began to feel at home in the Netherlands. Anne and Margot made a number of friends, not just Dutch ones but German ones as well, as more and more refugees came to live in the neighborhood. Many more Jews, including Anne's uncles Julius and Walter Holländer, fled Germany, especially after Kristallnacht.* During the years that the Frank family lived safely in the Netherlands, Hitler built up a large army. On September 1, 1939, Germany attacked Poland. That meant war. Would Germany attack the Netherlands as well? Hitler had said that he would not, but many people feared that he would go back on his word. Jews in particular were afraid, for they knew what had happened in Germany.

→

February 1934. Margot tries out the new roller skates she has been given for her birthday.

Summer 1934. Margot, Anne, and Edith Frank having ice cream on Zandvoort beach. Sitting in the beach chair is Mrs. Schneider, Otto Frank's former secretary from Frankfurt, who was visiting the Frank family.

Anne and Margot in the summer of 1934. The Frank family often went to the beach.

← Anne in the second form of
the Montessori school, Miss
Baldal's class

Anne, 1935

Anne with her friend Sanne Ledermann outside their house in
Merwedeplein, 1935

→

In September 1935 Anne
and Grammy Frank were
staying with relatives in Sils-
Maria, Switzerland.

Sept. 1935

in Sils - Maria

July 1936. Anne playing with her friends Eva Goldberg and Sanne Ledermann in Merwedeplein

Now and then Anne went with her mother to visit her father at work. Here, she is standing on the steps outside Otto Frank's business.

Anne and Margot with their mother, 1936

→

Sometimes Grandma went down to the beach. This photograph was taken in the summer of 1939 in Zandvoort. Anne pasted it into her diary three years later, adding: **This is the only photograph of Grandma Holländer, I think of her so often and wish she were still keeping the domestic peace. Margot and I had just come out of the sea and I still remember feeling terribly cold, and that is why I put on my bathrobe. Grandma was sitting behind us so sweetly and calmly. As she did so often.** (September 28, 1942)

Juni 1938

Anne with a baby rabbit in
Amstelrust park in Amsterdam
South, summer 1938

Anne verde-
digt een
gewezen burcht
tegen de op-
komende
zee.

← Anne defended the remains of a castle against the rising tide, as she noted later next to this photograph.

Anne celebrated her tenth birthday on June 12, 1939. From left to right: Lucie van Dijk, Anne Frank, Sanne Ledermann, Hanneli Goslar, Juultje Ketellapper, Kitty Egyedi, Mary Bos, Letje Swillens, and Martha van den Berg.

1940-1942

War and occupation[*]

After May 1940 the good times were few and far between: first there was the war, then the capitulation, and then the arrival of the Germans, which is when the trouble started for the Jews. Our freedom was severely restricted by a series of anti-Jewish decrees: Jews were required to wear a yellow star;[*] Jews were required to turn in their bicycles; Jews were forbidden to ride trolleys; Jews were forbidden to ride in cars, even their own; Jews were required to do their shopping between 3:00 and 5:00 p.m.; Jews were required to frequent only Jewish-owned barbershops and beauty salons; Jews were forbidden to be out on the streets between 8:00 p.m. and 6:00 a.m.; Jews were forbidden to attend theaters, cinemas, or any other forms of entertainment; Jews were forbidden to use swimming pools, tennis courts, hockey fields, or any other athletic fields; Jews were forbidden to go rowing; Jews were forbidden to take part in any athletic activity in public; Jews were forbidden to sit in their gardens or those of their friends after 8:00 p.m.; Jews were forbidden to visit Christians in their homes; Jews were required to attend Jewish schools, etc. You couldn't do this and you couldn't do that, but life went on.

(June 20, 1942)

On May 10, 1940, the German army invaded the Netherlands, despite Hitler's promise not to do so. Five days later, the Germans bombed the center of Rotterdam, and the Dutch army gave up the unequal struggle.

When Anne's birthday came around a month later, there were no celebrations since no one was in a festive mood. As expected, the Jews were first to be turned on. To begin with all civil servants had to sign an "Aryan declaration";* next, all Jews had to register. Those who failed to do so could be sentenced to five years in jail. As a result, it did not take the Nazis long to know exactly who was a Jew and where each one lived.

As we can see from Anne's diary, more and more anti-Jewish measures continued to be passed. By June 1942, the list of prohibitions was so long that Anne tired of listing them all.

→

Anne playing with Hanneli Goslar, a neighbor's daughter in Merwedeplein. Hanneli was in Anne's class at school, and her parents were friends of Otto and Edith Frank. It is May 1940.

Margot (wearing sunglasses) and classmates on the tennis court during the summer of 1940. A little over a year later Jews were forbidden to be members of bridge, dancing, or tennis clubs.

Anne and Margot in August 1940. One year later Jews were forbidden to use the beach.

Anne and Margot often sunbathed on the flat roof of their house.

In the winter of 1940, Anne
attended the fifth form of
the Montessori school.

Anne at the writing desk
in their house in Merwedeplein, 1941

Summer 1941. Anne on
a visit to her friend Sanne
Ledermann

Anne, Raymond, en Sanne Ledermann

←

The Frank family in front of their
house in Merwedeplein in May 1941.
At that stage, the Netherlands had
been occupied by the German army
for a year.

Anne in the sixth form of the Montessori
school. Following the summer holidays
in 1941 she was due to attend a separate
school for Jewish children. The Nazis did
not want Jewish and non-Jewish children
to attend the same school.

Mei 1935  Dec. 1935 Mei 1936 Dec. 1936

Mei 1937  Mei 1938  Mei 1939

Mei 1940  Mei 1941  Mei 1942

Mei 1935

Dec. 1935

Mei · '36

Mei 1937

Mei 1938

Mei 1939

Mei 1940

Mei 1941

Mei 1942

1942-1944

In hiding

The 1942 summer holidays had started. On the morning of Saturday, July 5, Anne's friend Hello Silberberg came over. They sat on the balcony to chat. When Hello had to leave a little later, he promised to return in the afternoon. At three o'clock the doorbell rang. Anne thought it must be Hello, but it was the mailman. From that moment on everything in the life of Anne and her family changed.

The mailman had brought a call-up notice for Margot. She was to report for work in Germany. Margot was just sixteen and no one knew what would happen to her in Germany. One thing was clear: Margot would not be going!

Anne's father and mother had seen this coming, which was why they had prepared a secret hiding place—not just for their own family, but also for Hermann van Pels, his wife, Auguste, and their son, Peter. Hermann van Pels was a fellow director of Otto Frank's company. The Van Pelses were also Jewish. Anne's parents had originally planned to go into hiding on July 16, but under the circumstances they decided to disappear the very next day.

Anne's mother went to see Hermann van Pels right away, having told Anne and Margot to pack a few things as fast as they could. Anne crammed everything into her satchel: her diary, her curlers, handkerchiefs, schoolbooks, a comb, and some old letters. She kept worrying about going into hiding.

Hiding… where would we hide? In the city? In the country? In a house? In a shack? When, where, how… ? These were questions I wasn't allowed to ask, but they still kept running through my mind. … Preoccupied by the thought of going into hiding, I stuck the craziest things in the satchel, but I'm not sorry. Memories mean more to me than dresses. (July 8, 1942)

After a short while, Anne's mother returned with Hermann van Pels. No sooner were they inside the house than the doorbell rang again. This time it was indeed Hello Silberberg. Anne's mother sent him away, saying that Anne had no time right then. Hello looked surprised and disappointed. A moment later the telephone rang and Jacqueline Maarssen asked if Anne was in. Jacqueline was Anne's best friend. They chatted for a few moments, but Anne kept it short. She was afraid of giving the game away, since she could not, of course, breathe a word about their plans to anybody.

Hermann van Pels left to fetch Miep Gies. Miep worked in Otto Frank's office and knew all about their plan. She now carried a suitcase packed with clothes to the hiding place. Later, she returned with her husband, Jan, the two of them bringing even more clothes and shoes to the hiding place. Johannes Kleiman, another of Otto Frank's business colleagues, had also been alerted and came to take as many other belongings as possible away with him.
It was late when Anne finally went to bed.
I was exhausted, and even though I knew it'd be my last night in my own bed, I fell asleep right away. (July 8, 1942)

The Frank family got up at five thirty the next morning.

The four of us were wrapped in so many layers of clothes it looked as if we were going off to spend the night in a refrigerator, and all that just so we could take more clothes with us. No Jew in our situation would dare leave the house with a suitcase full of clothes. I was wearing two vests, three pairs of pants, a dress, and over that a skirt, a jacket, a raincoat, two pairs of stockings, heavy shoes, a cap, a scarf and lots more. I was suffocating even before we left the house, but no one bothered to ask me how I felt. (July 8, 1942)

At home, they left a piece of paper around with an address in Maastricht on it. If anyone found it, the Franks hoped they would think that the family had gone there, or perhaps to their relatives in Switzerland. They put a letter in their neighbor's mailbox as well, asking him to be kind enough to look after Moortje, the cat.

At about seven thirty Miep Gies rang the doorbell. She and Margot cycled to the hiding place. Because Jews were not allowed to use bicycles, Margot removed the Jewish star from her coat. Anne and her parents followed on foot.

So there we were, Father, Mother, and I, walking in the pouring rain, each of us with a satchel and a shopping bag filled to the brim with the most varied assortment of items. The people on their way to work at that early hour gave us sympathetic looks; you could tell by their faces that they were sorry they couldn't offer us some kind of transport; the conspicuous yellow star spoke for itself.

(July 9, 1942)

It was only when they were on their way that Anne learned where their hiding place was: in a disused part of her father's business at 263 Prinsengracht. Otto Frank, Hermann van Pels, and Johannes Kleiman had helped to turn the empty premises at the back of their business into a hiding place over the previous few months, filling it with furniture and food supplies.

When Anne and her parents arrived in Prinsengracht, Margot was waiting for them. The hiding place was not quite ready yet: boxes full of belongings were piled every-where. Anne and her father set to work right away. First they made curtains so that nobody could see inside. Then they began to unpack and tidy up. Anne's mother and Margot were too tired and miserable to help. But the next day they were feeling better and the four of them did some more cleaning up. In her diary, Anne told "Kitty":

Until Wednesday, I didn't have a chance to think about the enormous change in my life. Then for the first time since our arrival in the Secret Annex, I found a moment to tell you all about it and to realize what had happened to me and what was yet to happen. (July 10, 1942)

Anne liked their hiding place very much.

The Annex is an ideal place to hide in. It may be damp and lopsided, but there's probably not a more comfortable hiding place in all Amsterdam. No, in all of Holland. (July 11, 1942)

Just four of Otto Frank's colleagues and employees knew about the hiding place: Johannes Kleiman, Miep Gies, Victor Kugler, and Bep Voskuijl. There were other people working for the company in the warehouse on the ground floor. They could not suspect anything, for the fewer the people who knew about the hiding place, the less the chances of discovery.

The first few exciting days were followed by calmer weeks and months. Anne came to realize more and more that her carefree life was over.
Not being able to go outside upsets me more than I can say, and I'm terrified our hiding place will be discovered and that we'll be shot. (September 28, 1942)

One month earlier, she had been celebrating her birthday with all her friends, and now she was cooped up all day in a small room. She missed her girlfriends terribly. She also missed Moortje, the cat. When she peered out through the curtains, she occasionally saw a black cat that reminded her of Moortje roaming around in the garden. Then she felt very lonely and unhappy.

Anne had to be as quiet as a mouse all day so that the people working in the warehouse during the day would not suspect that there were people hiding in the Annex. Only in the evenings and on weekends, when no workers were around, could the people cooped up in the Annex leave their hideout.

Then they could wash in the office kitchen, for instance, and listen to the radio in the private office. Anne found that quite frightening.

Last night the four of us went down to the private office and listened to England on the wireless. I was so scared someone might hear it that I literally begged Father to take me back upstairs. Mother understood my anxiety and went with me. Whatever we do, we're afraid the neighbors might hear or see us. (July 11, 1942)

At night, too, Anne was often scared. If there was a thunderstorm or if the Germans were firing at Allied airplanes, she made straight for her father's bed. It was only there that she felt safe. On one occasion the gunfire was so loud that Anne was afraid to get back into her own bed. She fetched her blankets and lay down on the floor next to her father's bed.

Six weeks after the Franks went into hiding, the rest of the company arrived in the Secret Annex: Hermann and Auguste van Pels and their fifteen-year-old son, Peter. They brought their cat, Mouschi, along as well. Anne knew Peter well. He had been there on her thirteenth birthday and had given her a present.

Peter van Pels arrived at nine thirty in the morning (while we were still at breakfast). Peter's going on sixteen, a shy, awkward boy whose company won't amount to much. (August 14, 1942)

Even so, she liked the idea that she now had more people to talk to.

The black-and-white photographs on the following pages were taken a few years after the war by Maria Austria.

1. The front of Otto Frank's business premises in Prinsengracht (third from left). When you stand in front of the building, you would never think that there is another entire building at the back.

2. The people working in the warehouse knew nothing about the hiding place at the back. The photograph shows the front of the warehouse with the door to the street.

3. The staircase the helpers climbed every day. It opens onto the landing in front of the movable bookcase.

4/5. The movable bookcase hid the entrance to the Annex.

6. The only window in Anne Frank's small room. The curtains were always drawn. Sometimes Anne would peer outside through a chink.

7. Anne's room, which she had to share with Fritz Pfeffer. The door leads to the washroom.

8. The washroom and toilet were next to the small room Anne Frank shared with Fritz Pfeffer. During the day, the people in the Annex flushed the toilet as little as possible because the waste pipes ran through the warehouse.

9. The communal living and dining room was also the bedroom of Hermann and Auguste van Pels.

10. The entrance to the attic was by way of the stairs in Peter's room.

11. Anne and Peter spent a great deal of time together in the attic.

The rear of Otto Frank's business premises. The hiding place occupied the three upper stories.

1   Anne and Margot's room. Later Anne shared this room with Fritz Pfeffer. Margot then moved into her parents' room.

2   Otto and Edith Frank's bedroom.

3   Hermann and Auguste van Pels's bedroom.
    The warehouse was on the ground floor and Otto Frank's private office (right) and the kitchen belonging to the business (left) were on the first floor. The people in hiding only went there once all the workers had gone home.

The people in the Annex shared all their meals, and after two days they felt like one big family. When the workers in the warehouse broke for lunch, the helpers often came up to the hiding place from the office to eat as well. The "residents" welcomed their company. That way they heard the latest news from outside. But the news was often far from good. Anne heard from Bep Voskuijl that a girl in her class had been deported* to Poland. Like Margot, more and more Jews were being called up for work in Germany. Most of them failed to report. That is why the Nazis organized razzias, or raids*: they would close off a street or a district and search all the houses. Any Jews they discovered were arrested. Then—just like Anne's classmate—they were taken off by train to concentration camps. Everyone feared that the prisoners would come to grief in the end.

We assume that most of them are being murdered. The English radio says they're being gassed. Perhaps that's the quickest way to die. I feel terrible. (October 9, 1942)

The seven people hidden away in the Annex lived in constant fear of being discovered. Then their helpers managed to think of a way of concealing the entrance to their hiding place more effectively. Bep Voskuijl's father built a movable bookcase and mounted it in front of the original gray door. It took those hiding beyond the door quite some time to get used to this strange new device.

After the first three days we were all walking around with bumps on our foreheads from banging our heads against the low doorway. Then Peter cushioned it by nailing a towel stuffed with wood shavings to the door frame. Let's see if it helps! (August 21, 1942)

The occupants of the Annex were crammed together and could never go out. That was hard on them all, but particularly on Anne. She missed her freedom terribly. On top of that, Mr. and Mrs. van Pels often found fault with her, which greatly annoyed Anne.

I have no intention of taking their insults lying down. I'll show them that Anne Frank wasn't born yesterday. They'll sit up and take notice and keep their big mouths shut when I make them see they ought to attend to their own manners instead of mine. . . . Am I really as bad-mannered, headstrong, stubborn, pushy, stupid, lazy, etc., etc., as that lot upstairs say I am? No, of course not. I know I have my faults and shortcomings, but they blow them all out of proportion! If you only knew, Kitty, how I seethe when they scold and mock me. It won't be long before I explode with pent-up rage. (September 28, 1942)

Worse still, Anne kept quarreling with her mother and she couldn't even see eye to eye with Margot all the time. The only person with whom she was on really good terms was her father. He understood her and she looked up to him. Anne told him that she liked him better than she did her mother. Otto Frank told her that was bound to change as she got older.

But they didn't quarrel in the Secret Annex all the time.

Mother, Margot, and I are once again the best of friends. It's actually a lot nicer that way. Last night Margot and I were lying side by side in my bed. It was incredibly cramped, but that's what made it fun. She asked if she could read my diary once in a while. "Parts of it," I said and asked about hers. She gave me permission to read her diary as well.... I once asked Margot if she thought me ugly. She said that I was okay and had nice eyes. A little vague, don't you think? (October 14,1942)

Anne was surprised to discover that she could sit still for such long periods of time.

We're as still as baby mice. Who would have guessed three months ago that quicksilver Anne would have to sit so quietly for hours on end, and what's more that she could? (October 1, 1942)

During the day, Anne was generally busy doing the homework her father had assigned her. Otto Frank did not want Margot and Anne to fall too far behind with their schoolwork. Anne was particularly interested in history. She loved reading about the Greek and Roman gods. Sometimes she helped Miep Gies and Bep Voskuijl with their office work. And then there were all sorts of household chores that had to be done every day, such as cooking and washing up. But when everything had been done, and Anne at last had time for herself, she liked to keep up her diary.

In November, an eighth person moved into the Secret Annex. Fritz Pfeffer was a Jewish acquaintance of the two families hiding there. He was a dentist. His girlfriend, Charlotte, was not Jewish and so did not have to go into hiding. Fritz Pfeffer had been married and had a son named Werner. He had sent Werner to England before the war. Fritz Pfeffer was put into Anne's room. Margot now had to sleep with her parents.

Just as we thought, Mr. Pfeffer is a very nice man. Of course, he didn't mind sharing a room with me; to be honest, I'm not exactly delighted at having a stranger use my things, but you have to make sacrifices for a good cause.... "If we can save even one of our friends, the rest doesn't matter," said Father, and he's absolutely right. (November 19, 1942)

Fritz Pfeffer brought them bad news. Raids were taking place all over the city, and Jews were being rounded up and packed off to concentration camps.

Countless friends and acquaintances have been taken off to a dreadful fate. Night after night, green and gray military vehicles cruise the streets. They knock on every door, asking whether any Jews live there. If so, the whole family is immediately taken away. If not, they proceed to the next house. It's impossible to escape their clutches unless you go into hiding....
No one is spared. The sick, the elderly, children, babies, and pregnant women—all are marched to their death. (November 19, 1942)

Anne kept wondering what was happening to her girl-friends. What dreadful things were being done to them? Were they still alive? Anne felt guilty about being safe and sound in the Annex.

I feel wicked sleeping in a warm bed, while somewhere out there my dearest friends are dropping from exhaustion or being knocked to the ground. I get frightened myself when I think of close friends who are now at the mercy of the cruelest monsters ever to stalk the earth. And all because they're Jews. (November 19, 1942)

The people in the Annex tried not to dwell on the miseries of the war all the time. On December 4, they celebrated Hanukkah, an important Jewish festival, and exchanged small presents. Next day, on St. Nicholas's Day, the helpers brought a hamper with presents and poems for everyone. They were given small presents in return. It was the first time Anne had celebrated St. Nicholas's Day. She thought it was even better than Hanukkah.

At first Anne thought Fritz Pfeffer very nice, but with the two of them sharing a very small room, things weren't easy. They quarreled more and more frequently.

Mr. Pfeffer, the man who was said to get along so well with children and to absolutely adore them, has turned out to be an old-fashioned disciplinarian and preacher of unbearably long sermons on manners. Since I have the singular pleasure (!) of sharing my far too narrow room with His Excellency, and since I'm generally considered to be the worst behaved of the three young people, it's all I can do to avoid having the same old scoldings and admonitions repeatedly flung at my head and to pretend not to hear. This wouldn't be so bad if Mr. Pfeffer weren't such a tattletale and hadn't singled out Mother to be the recipient of his reports. If Mr. Pfeffer's just read me the riot act, Mother lectures me all over again, this time throwing the whole book at me. And if I'm really lucky, Mrs. van P. calls me to account five minutes later and lays down the law as well! (November 28, 1942)

The rest of the company also had a lot to say about Anne's bad behavior. She poured out her heart to her diary:

I'd like to scream at Mother, Margot, the Van Pelses, Pfeffer, and Father too: "Leave me alone, let me have at least one night when I don't cry myself to sleep with my eyes burning and my head pounding. Let me get away, away from everything, away from this world!" … Everyone thinks I'm showing off when I talk, ridiculous when I'm silent, insolent when I answer, cunning when I have a good idea, lazy when I'm tired, selfish when I eat one bite more than I should, stupid, cowardly, calculating, etc., etc. All day long I hear nothing but what an exasperating child I am, and although I laugh it off and pretend not to mind, I do mind. I wish I could ask God to give me another personality, one that doesn't antagonize everybody. But that's impossible. I'm stuck with the character I was born with, and yet I'm sure I'm not a bad person. (January 30, 1943)

And so it was another year—1943. Throughout the Netherlands, Jews were being rounded up and packed off. The Nazis were determined to clear the whole country of its Jews. When Anne thought about that, she felt miserable and quite helpless. More and more often, Allied bombers were flying over Amsterdam at night, on their way to drop bombs on German towns and factories. Over the Netherlands, they were fired at by German anti-aircraft guns. It all terrified Anne.

I still haven't got over my fear of planes and shooting, and I crawl into Father's bed nearly every night for comfort. I know it sounds childish, but wait till it happens to you! The ack-ack guns make so much noise you can't hear your own voice. . . . I was shivering as if I had a temperature, and begged Father to relight the candle. He was adamant: there was to be no light. Suddenly we heard a burst of machine gun fire, and that's ten times worse than anti-aircraft guns. Mother jumped out of bed and, to Pim's [Father's] great annoyance, lit the candle. Her resolute answer to his grumbling was, "After all, Anne is not an ex-soldier!" And that was the end of that! (March 10, 1943)

Anne was full of admiration for everyone who helped people in hiding, because she knew what terrible risks they ran.

It's amazing how much these generous and unselfish people do, risking their own lives to help and save others. The best example of this is our own helpers. . . . Never have they uttered a single word about the burden we must be, never have they complained that we're too much trouble.

(January 28, 1944)   →

Auguste and
Hermann van Pels

Peter van Pels

Fritz Pfeffer

During the day, the helpers worked in the office. They tried to act as normal as possible, but they had to be on constant guard in case outsiders suspected that people were hiding in the Annex. This photograph was taken in 1941, that is, before the Franks and the Van Pelses went into hiding in the Annex. In the photograph: Victor Kugler (left) with Bep Voskuijl next to him. Miep Gies is sitting in front of the window. The two other women were no longer working in the office by the time the Frank family moved in.

Johannes Kleiman, one of the helpers, displays the entrance to the Secret Annex after the war.

The Frank family had a series of forty-eight passport photographs taken nearly every year. Anne cut some of these out, pasted them into her diary, and wrote brief commentaries about them.

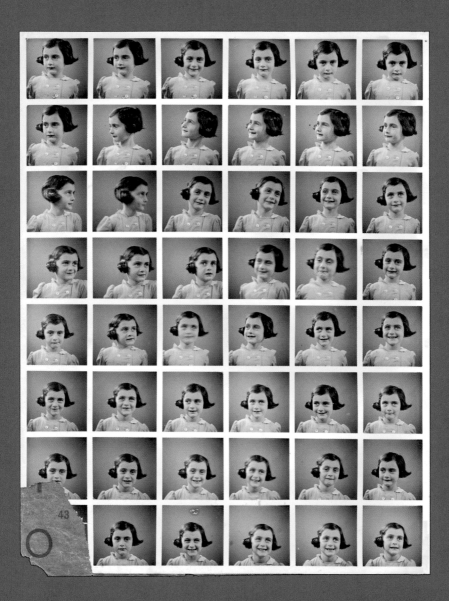

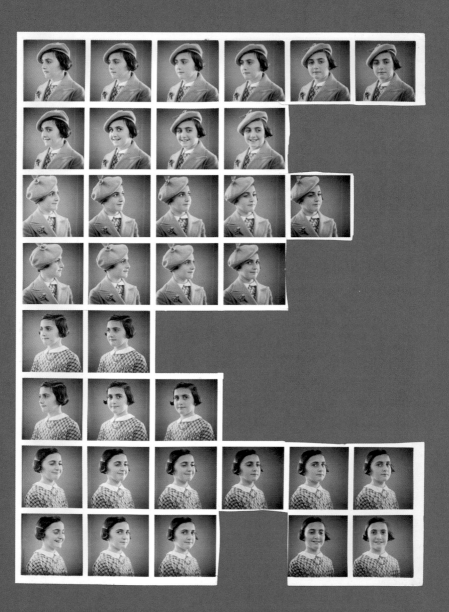

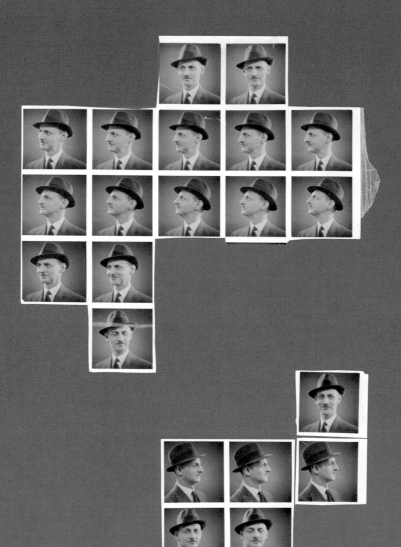

The helpers had various tasks: Johannes Kleiman and Victor Kugler ran the business and made sure that there was enough money to provide for those hiding in the Annex. Miep Gies and Bep Voskuijl saw to food, drink, clothing, and many other household essentials. Miep Gies often brought library books with her.

We long for Saturdays because that means books. . . . Ordinary people don't know how much books can mean to someone who's cooped up. Our only diversions are reading, studying, and listening to the wireless. (July 11, 1943)

The other helpers, too, quite often brought in books, newspapers, and magazines. Anne's favorite was *Cinema & Theatre*, a magazine that Victor Kugler brought her every week. The others thought it a waste of money, but they were constantly surprised by Anne's knowledge of films and film stars.

Bep Voskuijl had enrolled in a number of correspondence courses on behalf of the three young people, but under her own name. Margot, Peter, and Anne were taking a shorthand course. Shorthand is a way of quickly writing down what people are saying by using special signs. At first, Anne was very interested in shorthand—it seemed just like a secret language. But she soon dropped it again because she wanted to spend time on other subjects. On top of that, her eyes had started to act up. She needed to be fitted with glasses. *Ugh, won't I look like a muggins!*, she wrote in her diary. (July 11, 1943)

Miep was willing to take her to a specialist who could be trusted. Anne was terrified of walking down the street, though the thought of going out at long last greatly appealed to her. In preparation, she took her gray coat out of the wardrobe, but noticed that it had become much too small! The whole idea was dropped in the end, because everyone felt that the risks were too great. On top of that, they all believed that the war would soon be over.

In the meantime, Otto Frank continued to do all sorts of work for his company behind the scenes. Victor Kugler and Johannes Kleiman discussed all important business matters with him. One day some business associates from Germany came over to discuss Opekta deliveries. Otto Frank would dearly have liked to be present at the talks being held in the private office. That was, of course, out of the question, but if he lay down and pressed his ear to the floor above the office, he could hear everything they were saying below. He asked Margot to listen in as well because two ears were better than one. The German visitors arrived in the morning. Margot and her father lay listening on the floor until noon. The talks continued in the afternoon, but Otto Frank found it too difficult to carry on in his uncomfortable position. Anne took his place, but the conversation was so boring that she soon fell asleep. Because she did not want there to be the slightest sound, Margot did not dare to wake her up. It took half an hour before Anne awoke with a start. *Luckily Margot had paid more attention,* she wrote in her diary. (April 1, 1943)

On June 12, 1943, Anne turned fourteen. It was her first birthday in the Secret Annex. Her father presented her with a splendid poem, and everyone else brought her lovely presents, including a book on Greek and Roman mythology. Anne felt that sometimes it was best to be the youngest, because the other occupants of the Annex were not nearly so spoiled on their birthdays.

And so the days, the weeks, and the months went by. Sometimes the occupants of the Annex dreamed about what they would do first when they were free again.

Margot and Mr. van Pels wish, above all else, to have a hot bath, filled to the brim, which they can lie in for more than half an hour. Mrs. van Pels would like a cake, Pfeffer can think of nothing but seeing his Charlotte, and Mother is dying for a cup of real coffee. Father would like to visit Mr. Voskuijl, Peter would go into town, and as for me, I'd be so overjoyed I wouldn't know where to begin. Most of all I long to have a home of our own, to be able to move around freely, and have someone to help me with my homework again, at last. In other words, to go back to school!

(July 23, 1943)

They had now been cooped up in the Annex for more than a year. Anne often felt down in the dumps, because of the hopeless situation but also because of her own short-comings. Although she kept promising herself to stop being so disagreeable, she did not always succeed. She decided to react differently to the things she found a bore.

I don't think my opinions are stupid but other people do, so it's better to keep them to myself. I apply the same tactic when I have to eat something I loathe. I put the dish in front of me, pretend it's delicious, avoid looking at it as much as possible, and it's gone before I've had time to realize what it is. When I get up in the morning, another very disagreeable moment, I leap out of bed, think to myself, "You'll be slipping back under the covers soon," walk to the window, take down the blackout screen, sniff at the crack until I feel a bit of fresh air, and I'm awake. I strip the bed as fast as I can so I won't be tempted to go back in. Do you know what Mother calls this sort of thing? The art of living. Isn't that a funny expression? (August 10 ,1943)

In the summer of 1943, Anne discovered just how much she loved writing. From that moment on, she not only kept her diary but also started writing short stories. One of these was called "The Best Little Table," and was about a big fight she had had with Fritz Pfeffer. Their room contained a small table, at which Anne often used to work and keep her diary. But Fritz Pfeffer also wanted the table to do his studies. He was learning Dutch and Spanish. Anne was allowed to use the table every day from two thirty to four o'clock while Fritz Pfeffer was having a nap. For the rest of the day, she never went into the room. She asked him very politely if she might not have the use of the small table twice a week from four to five thirty. But Fritz Pfeffer wouldn't hear of it, and went on to accuse her of all sorts of things. Anne was furious.

For one fleeting moment I thought, "Him and his lies, I'll smack his ugly mug so hard that he'll go bouncing off the wall!" But the next moment I thought, "Calm down, he's not worth getting so upset about!" (July 13, 1943)

She ran to her father to complain about Pfeffer and to ask him to have a word with her roommate. After a long discussion, Pfeffer agreed to let Anne have the table two afternoons a week. But he was so angry that he didn't speak to her for two days. Worse still, he didn't keep to the agreement, and regularly demanded the use of the table between five and five thirty. All very childish, Anne thought.

One night there was a noise in the office below. Still as mice and trembling with fear they all heard the sounds getting dangerously close. Were they about to be discovered? After a while, the noises stopped and they heard nothing more. To make quite certain, they kept absolutely still for a while longer. The next day it appeared that the office had been broken into. The helpers said that more and more people were taking to theft and burglary in desperation, as it became harder and harder to get enough food. Clothes and shoes, too, had become scarce and very expensive.

The fear of discovery and betrayal mounted when Willem van Maaren came to work in the warehouse in February 1943. Needless to say, he was told nothing about the people in hiding, but he kept asking awkward questions about the Annex.

Another fact that doesn't exactly brighten up our days is that Mr. van Maaren, the man who works in the warehouse, is getting suspicious about the Annex. . . . We wouldn't care what Mr. van Maaren thought of the situation except that he's known to be unreliable and to possess a high degree of curiosity. (September 16, 1943)

They decided to be extra careful and quiet during the day.

Anne was often downhearted and pale. "Goodness, you look awful," she was always being told. She had a particularly hard time on Sundays. The business was closed then and the helpers didn't come to the Annex in the afternoon, so that there were few diversions.

My nerves often get the better of me, especially on Sundays, that's when I really feel miserable. The atmosphere is stifling, sluggish, leaden. Outside you don't hear a single bird, and a deathly, oppressive silence hangs over the house and clings to me as if it were going to drag me into the deepest regions of the underworld. At times like these, Father, Mother, and Margot don't matter to me in the least. I wander from room to room, climb up and down the stairs, and feel like a songbird whose wings have been ripped off and who keeps hurling itself against the bars of is dark cage. "Let me out, where there's fresh air and laughter!" a voice within me cries. I don't even bother to reply anymore, but lie down on the divan. Sleep makes the silence and the terrible fear go by more quickly, helps pass the time, since it's impossible to kill it. (October 29, 1943)

Sometimes Anne peered through a gap in the curtain. Then she could see the garden with the chestnut tree and the back of the houses across the way. Some evenings, she watched the neighbors through binoculars.

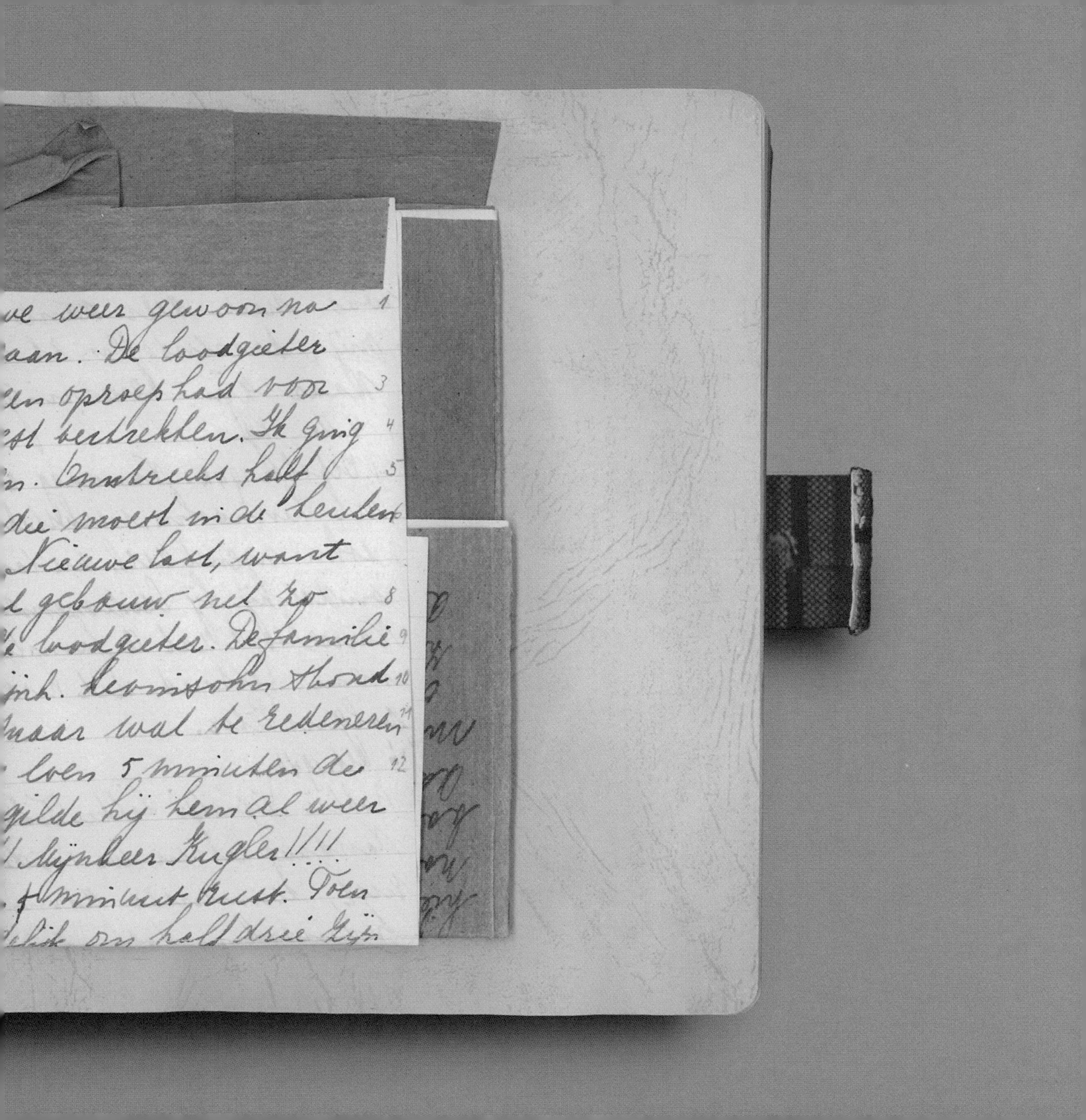

e weer gewoon na 1
aan. De loodgieter
en oproep had voor 3
st betrekken. Ik ging 4
n. Omstreeks half 5
die moest in de keuken
Nieuwe last, want
l gebouw niet zo 8
e loodgieter. De familie 9
inh. Levinsohn thond 10
naar wat te redeneeren
oen 5 minuten de 12
gilde hij hem al weer
l Mijnheer Kugler!!!!
f minuut rust. Toen
lik om half drie zijn

In de zomer van 1941 werd Oma Holländer erg ziek. Zij was toen al bij ons. Zij
moest geopereerd worden, en van mijn
verjaardag kwam niet veel.

In Maart 1940 ook niet, want toen was
de oorlog met haarbij in Nederland.

Deze winter 1941-1942 is Oma gestorven.
En niemand weet hoeveel ik aan haar
denk en nog van haar houdt.

Deze verjaardag 1942 is dan ook ge-
wijd om alles in te halen en Oma's
lichtje stond er naast.

                    Vrijdag 19 Juni 1942.

Vanochtend was ik thuis, ik heb heel
erg lang geslapen. Toen kwam Hanneli en hebben we nog wat gekletst.

Jacque is nu opeens erg met Ilse
ingenomen en doet erg kinderachtig
en flauw tegen mij, die valt mij hoe
langer hoe meer tegen. Anne

Dit is Juni 1939.
Dat is de eenige foto van 2
oma Hollander, aan
haar denk ik nog
zo vaak en ik wou
dat hij nog maar
de huiselijke vrede
bewaarde. Margot en
ik kwamen
toen net
uit het wa-
ter en ik
weet nog ik
had het erg
koud, daar-
om heb ik mijn
badjas om-
gedaan, om
zit er zo
lief en ve-
dig achter..
Hoals zij
zo vaak te
kijken heeft
Anne Frank
28 Sept. 194.

Dit is ook
in 1940,
nog eens
Margot en
ik. Ik bevou
mij maar met de
vacht dat Margot
op bovenstaande foto
1939 ook nog niet erg
ontwikkeld was. Hij
as toen net als ik nu
jaar en zelfs al ouder
Ik hoeft dus niet in dit geval
zo op mij neer te kijken. Anne Frank.
20 Sept. 1942.

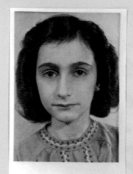

Ik begin met de foto
van Margot en eindig
met mijn eigen.
Dit is ook Januari
1942. Deze foto is
afschuwelijk, en ik
lijk er absoluut niet op.

Omi is in Zwitser-
land zij is een
erg lieve en
knappe vrouw, die
met al haar ken-
nissen vrienden
en familieleden
goed samen
komt en er ook
alles voor over
heeft. Zij woont
nu bij de zuster
van papi, tante
Leni en Stephan en

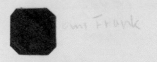

Anne Frank

1941.

Bernd. Omi is
ook altijd erg
aardig tegen
mij geweest.
zij is nu in 19
76 jaar en wij
hopen dat wij
haar na de oor-
log gezond weer

31

11 Mei 1939 heb ik deze snoezige brief van papi gekregen, het zal me een steun voor mijn leven zijn, tenminste als ik niet zoals Margot hem ergens zou laten liggen, zoals Margot hem & hu thuis heeft.

Prive'

KOOPT CULTUREELE EN SOCIALE ZORG ZOMERZEGELS

NEDERLAND

AMSTERDAM C.S. 18-19 11 V 1939

Mej. Anne Frank

Merwedeplein 37

Amsterdam

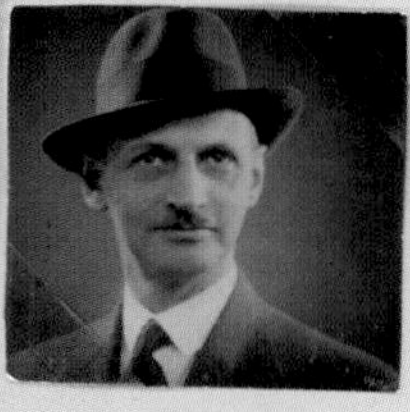

vie mijn dagboek schrijven. Mevr. Kleiman
en Bep en ook Bep Voskuijl hebben ons
zo geholpen, we hebben al rabarber,
aardbeien en kersen gehad, en ik denk
niet, dat we ons hier voorlopig zullen
vervelen.
Mevr. van Pels verteld het praatje dat papa
bevriend is met een oud kapitein uit het
leger en die heeft hem geholpen om naar
België te komen, die praatjes weet nu
iedereen en wij vermaken ons ermee.
Ik lezen lekken we ook en we hopen
nog een heleboel spelletjes.
Uit het raam kijken of naar buiten
gaan mogen wij natuurlijk nooit.
Ook moeten we zachtjes zijn, want beneden mogen ze ons niet horen.
Nu houd ik op want ik heb nog
veel te doen.

het verhaal wordt
ernstiger, maar is
↑ glimlach is een
grapje
er nog van het
ernstige gedeelte.
oh wat een
mop.
— wat zou er nou komen?
← ook lief
ddág, Jamij
gaat het
goed!"
(lachende
beleefdheid.)
het verhaal
is leuk

en ik ook
ervan mee-
gebruiken.

4 We doen

(bed of ee...

Beste Kitty,
De rokjes h...
horen hoe ...
is het soo...
zakken ge...
gesprongen...
ren al los...
overal wa...
den en d...
geval wat...
durven Ve...
rokje dat ik...
van f1.95. M...
zo'n geval...
heupen Ve...
bels dat ...
zijn nu wee...
verschrikk...
maar staan...
Het zijn allemaal vooranstaande mannen en ze
hebben gewoon in de krant geschreven wegens sa
botage dat kan natuurlijk niemand bewijzen. Als n
de een of andere man iets doet b.v. een Duitserdood
schieten of iets laten ontploffen en hij wordt nie
gevonden dan worden een stuk of J van die vooraa
staande mannen, dieer absoluut niets mee te make

vervolg vorige blz.

Gerbus de vriend van   Bep gaat
Woensdag weg met   nog een
leboel   andere
Neder-   landse
mensen-   Die stu-
ren ze nu ook bijna allemaal
naar Duitsland om te werken.
Zowel mannen als vrouwen.
Vanochtend zijn we weer alle-
maal op de Veegschaal geweest,
Margot weegt nu 120 pond
Moeder   "   " 124 "
Vader   "   " 141 "
Anne   "   " 87 "
Peter   "   " 134 "
Mevrouw   "   " 106 "
Meneer   "   " 150 "
Ik heb nu in de drie maanden
dat ik hier ben 17 pond toegeno-
men, enorm hè! Vanochtend ben
ik begonnen om een kathoteek
kastje van kantoor te sorteren

Maar dat
kan ons
niets sche

...n aan je

...1942

Die...sdag.

...oet je een
...nauw,da
...aardappel
...irect stuk
...kk ers wa
...hier was,e
...lange dra
...pen. Zo'n
...hebben
...uis een
...g goed is
...stof ook
...om de
...maal bob
...elijk. Er
...,dat nie
...gedaan,
Wat sabotage is

...shennen doodgeschoten. Dat doen ze natuurlijk

...zida en heeft Clara en Louis als kinderen.

...komt Saartje die is getrouwd met een

...ensioneerd officier en heeft ook 4 kinde- 3 3

Sophie, Betsy, Cateau, Coba. Dan is er 4

... een nichtje uit Parijs in het boek, Marie 5

...sabeth Sylvain, die een van de eersten is

... meedoet aan de vrouwen emancipatie.

... is de strijd die er geweest is om de

...ouw, dat die ook wilde studeren en de-

...lfde vechten hebben als de man. Want vroeger

... de vrouw niet getrouwd was kwam ze

...eedal als oude hardwerkende sul bij

...en van haar broers in huis. Ik heb nog

...ee kinderen vergeten Naatje die niet 14

...trouwd is een bij Abraham het huishou-

...n doet en Abraham die 12 kinderen heeft

...arvan 2 er al waren voor dat hij getrouwd

... mag Bep misschien vragen of zij bij

... eens kan gaan kijken of die nog dagboeken

...open, want anders moet ik gauw een schrift nemen,

...David die is ... en is getrouwd met (Rie).

16. Oct. 1942.
Vrijdag

Beste Jet,

Als Emmy een krabbel ertussen door krijgt, heb jij ook geen thiefhrid, dus hoe gaat er mee? Alweer een beetje van de schrik bekomen, ik hoop van wel. Hier is gelukkig nog alles bij het oude. Ik heb vandaag lijsten gemaakt van de Franse onregelmatige werkw. Het is een precies en vervelend werkje maar ik wil het graag afmaken. Ik heb nog niets aan Duro gedaan mis- schien maandavond nog. Maar het is Vrij- dag dus dat is critisch. Mama is weer in den rotbui. We hebben gehoord dat de familie Stohmke is gaan schuilen, geluk- kig maar. Ik ben nu Körner aan het lezen, die schrijft erg leuk. Nu tot de volgende keer Jetku-lief van

Anne Rang

anzo in
een Spiegel

Zo kijk ik in een kinder- wagen

Dik is ook snoezig hé.

Anne.

Hier heb ik zeker naar de harlekijn gekeken.

Anne

18 Oct. 1942
Zondg.

Lieve Marianne,   10 Oct. 194
gisteren is het   Zondag
schrijven er weer bij ingeschoten. Ten eerste omdat ik de lijst van Franse werkwoorden wil afmaken en ben tweede omdat ik ook nog ander werk had. Ik heb weer 3 boeken van Kleiman gekregen. De Arcadia. Dat han- delt over een reis naar Spit

6 De andere kant komt met een blauwe
zijurh met witte bont randjes voor met
8 Ritsluitingknahjes en ritsluiting in Clim-
huur met kas.

muts
fink

B.v. Hedwig, der
Vetter aus Brehem,
Hans Heilings Felsen,
Der Grüneh, Domino,
Die Gouvernante,
Der Vierjährige
Posten, Die Sühne,
Der kamf mit dem
Drachen, Der Nacht-
Wächter en zoal
meer. Vader wil dat
ik nu ook Hebbel en
andere boeken van
andere welbekende
Duitse schrijvers
ga lezen. Het Duits
lezen gaat nu al be-
trekkelijk vlot. Alleen
fluister ik het meestal, in plaats dat ik voor
mezelf lees. Maar dat gaat wel over. Gisteren heb

Dit is een
foto, zoals
ik me zou
wensen,
altijd zo
te zijn.
Dan had
ik nog wel een kans
om naar Holywood te
komen. Maar tegen-
woordig zie ik er
jammer genoeg mees-
tal anders uit.
Anne Frank.
10 Oct. 1942
Zondag.

ik weer wat
films heb ik
in de kamer
opgehangen,
maar nu
met foto-
hoekjes, dan
kan ik ze
er weer af-
halen. Bep
is gisteren
naar de
stad ge-
gaan en
heeft roe-
ken voor
Margot en
mij gekocht.
Maar ze
moeten weer
geruild, want
ze passen
niet hele-
maal.

Beste Phie...
Het is nu ...
geleden, d...
Schreven...
Van de we...
gelezen en...
gewerkt, 2...
het doen...
en zo zal...
ker verder...
Morgen ...
maar daar...
Wel over ...
der en ik...
laatste ...
ter met ...
vertrouwe...
got is kat...
vader he...
hij niet v...
mee wil ...
is toch al...
schat. Lev...
het ons nog altijd elke
dag lastig. Donderdag-
avond was ik beneden
met vader en heb in
Kuglers kantoor de
Debiteurenlijsten ge-
daan het was daar be-
neden erg eng, en ik
was blij toen het werk

Beste Pop,
We hebben gelukkig peulvruchten
gekregen 270 pond, maar het
personeel moet ook wat hebben.
We nemen nu in plaats van
land/stad levensmiddel kaarten land
stad
levensmiddel kaarten want dat
scheelt 7 gld. landkaarten kos-
ten h.l. maar 33 gld. en als wij
de broodbonnen die er op zit-
ten ook nog verkopen dan is
het nog maar 20 gld. Mijnh. v.
P. heeft nu haast geen geld
meer, Pim gelukkig wel. Mijnh.
Siemans (dat is onze bakker) krijgt
nu melksuiker en daarom le-
vert hij ons nu weer het brood
zonder bonnen voor de gewone
prijs. Kleiman is ook weer naar
Goldschmidt geweest maar hij
wil onze boel niet loslaten, en
hij zegt ook dat hij haast alles
voor Maatschappelijk doel weg-
gegeven heeft, maar dat geloof

...zag bene-
...het was
...kalk
...gevallen
...een blik
...oor ge-
...hu of
...als dat
...ik het
...V. P. maa...
...hengsel
...kan er
...com-
...een maar
...t. Ik ver-
...dan ooi...
...ik kan
...af wach-
...of 1 van
...Ik voel
...verlaten
...oom reel
...aards ge-
...is de ver-
...grauw,
...wat ik
doen zal. Sinds een paar
dagen is de kachel aan,
en de hele kamer staat
vol rook, ik houd toch veel
meer, van centrale verwar-
ming en daar zal ik de eni...
wel niet in zijn. Margot kan
ik niet anders betitelen als
een rotkind, dat mij dag en

allemaal

jammer van
de lelijke
tanden.

wil te
zeggen, misukt

leuk

deze foto
heb ik in
het groot
al een stukje
hier voor in-
geplakt

heft Hitler een rede va...
ng hebben we het kant...
van de verjaardag. Sla...
an juf van je liefheb...

AnneFrank

10 Nov. 1942.

Dinsdagavond

lijk weer overrompeld,
og eens over gesproken.
gg best één persoon op...
t lot heeft op mijnh...
die heeft niet zoveel
l met kugler ovenge...
nog eens een nachtje
besluit is eigenlijk al...
an opkijken, maar
an berichten als hij
earriveerd is. We zul...
mee kan brengen om...
want hij is tandarts, e...
j op de kamer slaap...
Vaarwel AnneFrank

hij moet de kathotheek
maken, daar komt d'...
Wij vonden dat veel...
zegt hij weer aan van...
len volgende week Do...
van der Hoe den dat...
Pfeffer met vragen bes...
kan het ook opvallen...
dag naar Miep en Jan...
brengt, want als Miep...
Wij ook weer in gevaar.
als Pfeffer vandaag ze...
oben en kan niet teg...
dan moet hij maar h...
als hij vandaag of mo...
eventueel ook in de...
dan kan hij ook niet...
heek nog opmaken en...
Miep weer met hem pr...
an de beslissing of hij...
en het dan zo tegele...
et bookkantoor moet...

1 Zaterdag 22 Januari 1944.

2 Ik vind het stom van mezelf dat ik al deze
  mooie ~~bladzijden door he~~ open heb gelaten,
4 maar het kan misschien geen kwaad als ik
  hierachter m'n algemene gedachten over het
6 geschrevene ~~heerpen~~.
7 Nu ik 1½ jaar later m'n dagboek weer inkijk,
8 verbaas ik me erg dat ik ooit zo'n on~~bedorven~~
9 bakvis ben geweest. Onwillekeurig weet ik,
10 dat hoe graag ik het zou willen ik zó nooit
11 meer zal kunnen worden. De buien de uitla-
12 tingen over Margot, Moeder en Vader begrijp
  ik nog net zo goed alsof ik ze gisteren heb
14 geschreven, maar dat ik zo ongegeneerd over
15 andere dingen geschreven heb kan ik me
  niet meer indenken.
  Ik schaam me werkelijk als ik de bladzijden
  lees die over onderwerpen handelen die ik het
  liefst mooier me voorstel.

Ik heb het zo onfijn neergeschr...
ja nu genoeg hiervan.
Wat ik ook goed begrijp is he...
en verlangen naar Moortje. ...
maar nog veel vaker onbewu...
die tijd dat ik hier was e...
langen naar vertrouwe...
kozingen. Dit verlangen...
en soms zwakker, ma...

hier had ik
een gebit zonder tanden aanen

ben
daarom
ook oer-lelijk.

Anne was given pills for her low spirits. She herself thought that laughter was a much better medicine. But then there was little to laugh about in the Annex, where the pressures of the war were felt every day and everyone lived in constant fear of discovery. They quarreled a lot among themselves. Anne sometimes felt that she couldn't keep up with it all: who was fighting with whom, and which quarrels had been discussed and settled.

Anne had a plan to improve the atmosphere in the Secret Annex. She remembered how nice it had been when they had celebrated St. Nicholas's Day the year before. She set to work with her father and produced a small present and a St. Nicholas's Day verse for everyone in the Annex. They took one shoe from each person and put a present in it. All the shoes went into a large basket. Anne's little plan really worked: everybody had a pleasant surprise and all their worries were momentarily forgotten.

But when Anne heard stories about what was happening outside, she felt sad again, for instance when Mrs. Kleiman talked to them about her daughter's hockey club or school plays. It was at such times that Anne realized how much she was missing. Though she knew that she ought not to be ungrateful, she found it hard not to be.

Whenever someone comes in from outside, with the wind in their clothes and the cold on their cheeks, I feel like burying my head under the blankets to keep from thinking, "When will we be allowed to breathe fresh air again?" I can't do that—on the contrary, I have to hold my head up high and put a bold face on things, but the thoughts keep coming anyway. Not just once, but over and over. Believe me, if you've been shut up for a year and a half, it can get too much for you sometimes. But feelings can't be ignored, no matter how unjust or ungrateful they seem. I long to ride a bike, dance, whistle, look at the world, feel young, and know that I'm free, and yet I can't let it show. Just imagine what would happen if all eight of us were to feel sorry for ourselves or walk around with the discontent clearly visible on our faces. Where would that get us? (December 24, 1943)

Then it was Christmas. Anne, Margot, and Peter were each given a pot of yogurt by the office helpers as a small Christmas present. It had been a long time since they last tasted yogurt. All the adults were given a bottle of beer. Miep Gies had baked a special Christmas cake, decorated with the words "Peace 1944."

In January 1944, Anne was leafing through her diary and was shocked by all the unpleasant things she had written about her mother. She resolved to stop quarreling with her mother and to keep her mouth shut when her mother annoyed her. Anne noticed that her mother was doing the same. As a result things between them improved considerably.

Anne realized that she had changed a great deal over
the past few months.

Then during the second half of 1943, I became a young woman, an adult in body, and my mind underwent a great, a very great change, I came to know God! I started to think, to write, and I discovered myself. I gained in confidence but also in sorrow because I realized that I no longer cared for Mother, and that Father would never become my confidant. (March 7, 1944)

Anne discovered that she had grown much wiser. She
was still boisterous and bold and always had something
disparaging to say about everybody. But according to
her that was just on the surface. The others could not see
beyond that, but "inside" she had changed. She now knew
her good and her bad qualities and also the many things
that really mattered to her. That is why she thought it a
great bore that the grownups went on treating her like a
child.

Even though I'm only fourteen, I know what I want, I know who's right and who's wrong, I have my own opinions, ideas, and principles, and though it may sound odd coming from a teenager, I feel I'm more of a person than a child—I feel I'm completely independent of others. (March 17, 1944)

Anne had learned to look at things afresh. Thus while she
used to think that Mr. and Mrs. van Pels started all the
quarrels in the Annex, she now realized that her parents
were also to blame.

Anne would have loved to have someone to talk to about all the things she had on her mind. One day she offered to help Peter with his crossword puzzle. That gave her a good excuse to go into his room. Anne knew perfectly well how shy he was and how hard he found it to talk about himself. She had trouble with that as well and realized it didn't do her any good. In her diary, she asked "Kitty":

Can you tell me why people go to such lengths to hide their real selves? Or why I always behave very differently when I'm in the company of others? Why do people have so little trust in one another? I know there must be a reason, but sometimes I think it's horrible that you can't ever confide in anyone, not even those closest to you. (January 22, 1944)

At night, Anne dreamed about another Peter, about Peter Schiff, whom she had had a crush on before she went into hiding. In her dream they embraced. For a moment she could feel his cheek against hers, but then she woke up. After that dream she kept thinking about Peter Schiff. That made her feel less lonely and a little bit happier.

Anne would now go to Peter van Pels's room as often as she could. They talked a great deal about their plans for the future. After the war, Peter wanted to emigrate to the Dutch East Indies and work on a plantation there. Anne started to dream about Peter van Pels. She wanted to spend the whole day with him.

→

A few years ago the Secret Annex was completely refurnished for a film. The color photographs of the rooms in the Annex on the following pages were taken on that occasion.

Otto and Edith Frank's room. Anne's parents slept with Margot in this small room. Margot had to make do with a camp bed. The private office was right under this room.

Anne's small room, which she
had to share with Fritz Pfeffer

This is how the bathroom
must have looked at the
time.

The communal living and
dining room

Peter's room. Anne sometimes envied Peter because he had a room of his own.

The attic was chiefly used
for storing food, such as
beans and potatoes.

In the long run, she stopped seeing any difference between Peter van Pels and Peter Schiff. Anne was in love again! She discovered that she and Peter van Pels had a lot in common. Both of them felt rather insecure and were trying to find themselves. Both had a mother who did not understand them. But Anne also saw that there were differences between them. When she felt unsure of herself, she would come straight out with it, but when Peter was unsure of himself he would retire to his room.

Sometimes Anne had a real need to be left alone.

Last night I went downstairs in the dark. . . . I stood at the top of the stairs while German planes flew back and forth, and I knew I was on my own, that I couldn't count on others for support. My fear vanished. I looked up at the sky and trusted in God. (January 30, 1944)

Anne believed that nature could help to make people happy. By this time she had not been outdoors for more than one and a half years. All she could see of nature was the sky and the old chestnut tree in the garden. Some nights she went down into the office to look at the moon and the stars through the window. She believed that helped to fight her dark moods better than pills could. Anne's mother often told her to remember that there were many people who were worse off. Anne did not think that was a great help. She believed that you have to find happiness inside you and not by comparing your own situation with the misery of others. Anne often tried to share her ideas and feelings with Margot, but she did not find her as easy to talk to as Peter.

Her talks with Peter helped to make her life in the Annex more
bearable. On the evening of Saturday, March 18, Anne went to
see Peter again. They went up to the attic.

He was standing on the left side of the open window, so I went over to the right side. It's much easier to talk next to an open window in semi-darkness than in broad daylight, and I think Peter felt the same way. We told each other so much, so very much, that I can't repeat it all. But it felt good; it was the most wonderful evening I've ever had in the Annex. (March 19, 1944)

The adults were curious about what Peter and Anne had
to talk about, and made feeble jokes on the subject.

On the evening of Sunday, April 9, there was another break-
in. It was the umpteenth burglary but this time the panic
was greater than ever before. A large panel was missing from
the warehouse door, and someone had apparently called
the police, who arrived a little while later and searched the
building.

Then, at eleven fifteen, a noise below. Up above you could hear the whole family breathing. For the rest, no one moved a muscle. Footsteps in the house, the private office, the kitchen, then. . . . on the staircase. All sounds of breathing stopped, eight hearts pounded. Footsteps on the stairs, then a rattling at the bookcase. This moment is indescribable. "Now we're done for," I said, and I had visions of all fifteen of us being dragged away by the Gestapo* that very night. More rattling at the bookcase, twice. Then we heard a tin fall, and the footsteps receded. We were out of danger, so far! A shiver went through everyone's body, I heard several sets of teeth chattering, no one said a word. (April 11, 1944)

They did not close an eye for the rest of the night. They were
terrified that the police might have discovered something and
that they would be back. But all ended well this time.

In the weeks that followed Anne and Peter often sought
each other out.

What could be nicer than sitting before an open window, enjoying nature, listening to the birds sing, feeling the sun on your cheeks, and holding a darling boy in your arms! (April 19, 1944)

Anne and Peter were in love.

At eight thirty I stood up and went to the window, where we always say good-bye. He came over to me, and I threw my arms around his neck and kissed him on his left cheek. I was about to kiss the other cheek when my mouth met his, and we pressed our lips together. In a daze, we embraced, over and over again, never to stop, oh! (April 28, 1944)

Anne wondered what her parents thought about her and
Peter and decided to talk to her father about it. When they
happened to be alone she said:

Father, I expect you've gathered that when Peter and I are together, we don't exactly sit at opposite ends of the room. Do you think that's wrong? (May 2, 1944)

Otto Frank was startled, and told her to be alone with
Peter less often. Anne disagreed completely with this
advice and continued to see Peter in his room every day.
Her father warned her again but Anne refused to listen.
Instead she wrote her father an angry letter, telling him to
trust her and not to keep treating her as a little child.

Writing became increasingly important to Anne.

The nicest part is being able to write down all my thoughts and feelings; otherwise, I'd completely suffocate. (March 16, 1944)

At the end of March they all listened to a memorable Dutch broadcast from London. When the war was over, the Dutch government wanted to gather diaries, letters, and other documents together in order to gain an idea of what it had really been like in the Netherlands during the war. The war must not be forgotten. The people hiding in the Annex thought of Anne's diary right away: the government was sure to want it. Anne gave her imagination free rein. What if she were to write a whole book about her life in the Secret Annex! But she was still unsure about her writing skills. Some of her short stories and certain parts of her diary struck her as well written, but others did not.

When I write I can shake off all my cares. My sorrow disappears, my spirits are revived! But, and that's a big question, will I ever be able to write something great, will I ever become a journalist or writer? I hope so, oh, I hope so very much, because writing allows me to record everything, all my thoughts, ideals, and fantasies. (April 5, 1944)

Anne tried to think of how she could turn her diary into a real book.

At long last, after a great deal of reflection, I have started my "Achterhuis" [Secret Annex]; in my head it is as good as finished, although it won't go as quickly as that really, if it ever comes off at all. (May 20, 1944)

She started to rewrite her diary on loose sheets of paper, covering four to five of them every day. Sometimes she wrote a whole new passage. She also left out some passages altogether, because they seemed either too childish or too personal to be included in her book.

Like everyone, Anne hoped that the war would not last
much longer.

One day this terrible war will be over. The time will come when we'll be people again and not just Jews! …We can never be just Dutch, or just English, or whatever, we will always be Jews as well. And we'll have to keep on being Jews, but then, we'll want to be. (April 11, 1944)

The war, which seemed to go on and on, gave Anne cause
for reflection.

What's the point of the war? Why, oh why can't people live together peacefully? Why all this destruction? …Oh, why are people so crazy? (May 3, 1944)

One day there was a fantastic piece of news on the radio.
It was June 6, 1944. Allied troops had landed in Normandy
in France, and were about to liberate all of occupied
Europe.

A huge commotion in the Annex! Is this really the beginning of the long-awaited liberation? The liberation we've all talked so much about, which still seems too good, too much of a fairy tale ever to come true? Will this year, 1944, bring us victory? We don't know yet. But where there's hope there's life. It fills us with fresh courage and makes us strong again. We'll need to be brave to endure the many fears and hardships and the suffering yet to come. It's now a matter of remaining calm and steadfast, of gritting our teeth and keeping a stiff upper lip! (June 6, 1944)

→

Anne stuck all sorts of
prints and photographs up
on the walls of her room to
make it look cozier.

THE LADY'S MAID
by
Maggie W. Turner

NORMA SHEARER

H.R.H. THE PRINCESS ELIZABETH OF YORK

H.R.H. THE PRINCESS MARGARET ROSE OF YORK

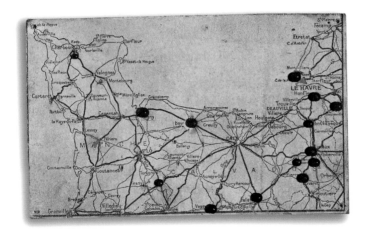

Those hiding in the Annex
could follow the Allied
advance on a map cut out
of a newspaper.

Otto and Edith Frank marked the
wall of their room with Margot and
Anne's heights during the period
they were in hiding.

→

29-7

27-5°

43 - 14-12   20-12

20-0

15-9 6-7

9-I   24-III

— 25 VII

24-11   9-III

10-1

8-12

18 IV

18-9 - 14

One week later Anne celebrated her birthday in the Annex for the second time. She was now fifteen, and everybody gave her presents. Miep Gies had bought Peter a bouquet of peonies to give to Anne, who was delighted with them. But she was even more delighted with the news that the invasion was going so well. The Allies were driving the Germans farther and farther back. Everyone in the Annex hoped that the war would be over by the end of the year.

In the weeks following her birthday, Anne thought a great deal about herself and about the people around her. Her father had turned out to be a disappointment. He did not take her seriously, did not treat her as a real person. When she complained, Otto told her that all her problems were due to her age and that they would pass, just as they did with other young girls. But her father told Anne so little about his own feelings that she lost her trust in him. That was why she stopped sharing her own worries with him, confiding them to her diary alone. But Anne was also disappointed in Peter. He had failed to become the friend she so badly needed. She could not talk to him as freely as she had thought at first. She gradually withdrew from him, but could not help noticing that he felt more and more drawn toward her.

Anne believed that young people were having a particularly hard time in the war. Adults, after all, could look back
on years of active life and feel sure of their opinions:

It's twice as hard for us young people to hold on to our opinions at a time when ideals are being shattered and destroyed, when the worst side of human nature predominates, when everyone has come to doubt truth, justice and God.... It's difficult in times like these: ideals, dreams, and cherished hopes rise within us, only to be crushed by grim reality. It's a wonder I haven't abandoned all my ideals, they seem so absurd and impractical. Yet I cling to them because I still believe, in spite of everything, that people are truly good at heart. It's utterly impossible for me to build my life on a foundation of chaos, suffering, and death. I see the world being slowly trans-formed into a wilderness, I hear the approaching thunder that, one day, will destroy us, too, I feel the suffering of millions. And yet, when I look up at the sky, I somehow feel that everything will change for the better, that this cruelty, too, will end, that peace and tranquility will return once more. In the meantime, I must hold on to my ideals. Perhaps the day will come when I'll be able to realize them! (July 15, 1944)

On August 1, 1944, Anne made her last entry in the diary.
Three days later, on Friday, August 4, what the people
hiding in the Secret Annex had been so afraid of all the
time came to pass…

1944-1945

The end

Friday, August 4 , 1944, seemed a day like any other. People were at work in the warehouse and in the office. In the Annex, they were quietly going about their business. It was a fine, warm summer's morning. At ten thirty a car suddenly stopped outside the entrance to 263 Prinsengracht. . . . Armed police got out and entered the ground floor of the warehouse. Somebody had telephoned the German police and told them that there were Jews in the building. The group in the Secret Annex had been betrayed.

The policemen went up the stairs to the office section. Victor Kugler was in his office and heard the noise on the stairs. He opened the door and saw four policemen, one of them in German uniform. *"Who is in charge here?"* a policeman snarled at him. *"I am,"* Victor Kugler replied calmly. The policemen then asked to see the storeroom. A moment later, they were standing by the movable bookcase. Without hesitation, the Dutch policemen swung the bookcase open. One of them pointed his revolver at Victor Kugler and ordered him to lead the way up. The first people he saw in the Annex were Edith and Margot Frank. They looked startled and could tell right away from Kugler's expression that something was wrong. Margot started to weep quietly. Fritz Pfeffer and Anne came out of their room to find out what was going on and were ordered to stand beside the other two with their hands above their heads. One of the policemen went up the stairs to the Van Pelses' room. Otto Frank was in Peter's room giving him an English lesson. Suddenly a man was standing there pointing a pistol at them. He ordered Otto Frank and Peter to go downstairs, where the rest of their group were standing with their hands up.

The Austrian SS officer, Karl Josef Silberbauer, was in charge. *"Where are your valuables?"* he asked curtly. Otto Frank pointed to the wardrobe. The officer then picked up Otto's briefcase and shook it out on the floor. Anne's diary, her notes, and all the loose pages fell out. The policemen then stuffed the jewelery and other valuables into the briefcase.

"Get ready," the SS man ordered. *"You have just five minutes."* Then his eyes fell on a soldier's footlocker.

"Where did you get that?" Silberbauer, a noncommissioned officer, asked in surprise. *"It's mine,"* Otto Frank replied. *"I was an officer in the German army during the Great War."* Silberbauer's attitude changed at once. In a much more friendly tone, he said, *"Take your time…"*

Despondently, they all collected their belongings.

When they had finished, they were ordered into the private office. There the helpers Johannes Kleiman and Victor Kugler sat waiting. They were questioned but refused to say anything. *"In that case, you'll have to come with us,"* said the SS man. Miep Gies insisted that she knew nothing about the hiding place. The Nazi let her go. Bep Voskuijl was sent out on some excuse by Johannes Kleiman and the policemen let her pass. One of the Dutch contingent rang the German headquarters and asked for a larger vehicle. They had obviously not counted on finding so many people.

After a while, a van drew up outside the office. The Jewish prisoners and the two helpers were ordered to get in. The van took them to German police headquarters, where they were locked up. Otto Frank was dismayed to find that Victor Kugler and Johannes Kleiman had been arrested as well. But Kleiman tried to put his mind at rest, and said that he did not regret the help he had given them.

When the van had left, Miep Gies and Bep Voskuijl made for the Annex to see if any of their friends' possessions could be recovered. The police had left everything in utter confusion. On the floor, they found Anne's diary, her exercise books, and a number of loose sheets of paper. They gathered up as many of these papers as they could and Miep locked them in the drawer of her desk. A few days later the Annex was emptied of all its remaining contents by the Amsterdam removal firm Puls. This firm cleared the houses of arrested Jews on German orders. The furniture and all other belongings were taken to Germany for distribution to German families.

On August 8, 1944, the eight Jews captured in the Secret Annex were put on a train to Westerbork, the transit camp for Jews. The doors of the train were locked. After more than two years they had their first glimpse of something other than their cramped, dark hiding place. Otto Frank noticed that Anne kept looking outside all the time. *"Anne could not be taken away from the window. It was summer outside. There were meadows and harvested cornfields. Villages flew by. The telephone wires bobbed up and down past the window."*

When the party arrived in Westerbork, they were registered. A card with personal data was made out for each of them. They were then housed in special punishment barracks. Jews who had been arrested for having gone into hiding were labeled "criminal cases" and treated with exceptional severity.

Anne and Margot were put in the same barracks as their mother. All their old quarrels were forgotten. Their father was in a separate barracks, but spent as much time as he could with his wife and daughters in the evenings. Once, when Anne was sick, he came around more often than usual and told her stories to take her mind off all her troubles. The Franks shared their barracks with Rosa de Winter, who had this to say about them: "Anne was happy in Westerbork, hard though it is to understand why, for we did not have it easy there. But Anne was really happy and seemed relieved because she had new people to talk to all the time. Margot was reticent, and Edith rarely spoke. Anne's father, too, was taciturn."

Anne, her mother, and Margot had to work all day with other women at a long table. They made friends with Janny Brille-slijper and her sister Lien. Janny later explained, "We had to break open batteries with a chisel and a hammer and then throw the pitch into one bin and the carbon rods into the other. The metal cap had to be wrenched off with a screwdriver and thrown into a third bin. We all got filthy and kept coughing a lot. Luckily we were allowed to talk to one another, because the work was very monotonous."

Otto and Edith Frank were constantly afraid. In particular, they feared deportation to one of the concentration camps. From Westerbork, crammed trains regularly carried prisoners to the East. No one knew exactly what went on there, but everyone feared the worst.

On September 2, 1944, the names of more than a thousand people due to leave the next day were read out. Everyone from the Annex was on that list, as were Janny and Lien Brilleslijper and Rosa de Winter. Next morning at ten, the train stood ready. It was not a passenger train but a freight train. More than seventy people were crammed into each car. "My God, are the doors really being shut now? Yes, they are. Shut on the herded, densely packed mass of people inside. Through narrow openings at the top we can see heads and hands, hands that will wave to us later when the train leaves. The train gives a piercing whistle. And 1,020 Jews leave Holland. This time the quota was really quite small, all considered: a mere thousand Jews, the extra twenty being reserves, for it is always possible, indeed quite certain this time, that a few will die or be crushed to death on the way. So many sick people and not a single nurse…" That is how Etty Hillesum described the departure of a train from Westerbork in a letter. That young Jewish woman had been packed off to Westerbork as well.

The long journey in the overcrowded train was horrific. Janny Brilleslijper has described it as follows: *The kindest, gentlest people became aggressive. When you have to stand for hours, you grow tired, terribly tired. All you want to do is to lean against something or to sit down. And when you finally manage to sit down, you get kicked and that makes you aggressive, it's only logical."* Anne and Margot were lucky. They could lean against their parents, but they could not get any sleep.

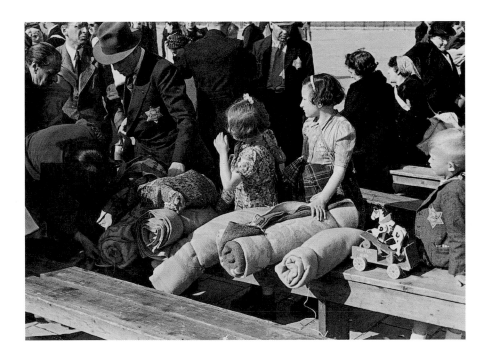

Jewish children and adults wait
at Muiderpoort railway station in
Amsterdam for the train that will
take them to Westerbork.

Jewish children in
Westerbork camp

Barracks in Westerbork.
Men and women are making
mattresses by filling old
postal bags with hay.

German officers on the
platform at Westerbork.
The train is about to leave.

Four women in a freight car traveling to one of the extermination camps in Eastern Europe.

Most of the prisoners carried a suitcase or bag packed with their possessions. Some hid gold and jewels in their clothes, but they were soon stripped of these. Rosa de Winter wrote: *"SS men stood by the door and held their caps under our noses. We had to put our money and valuables into them. Grinning, the guards ran to the next wagon with their filled caps. Then the journey continued."*

The train traveled on eastward. Sunday passed and night fell. A bucket in which seventy people had to relieve themselves stood in every wagon. The stench was horrific. *"On Monday morning, twenty of the prisoners were allowed to leave the train to fetch water and to have a bit of a wash,"* Lien Brilles-lijper remembered. *"The buckets were emptied as well. Then the doors were shut again. It was the last time we saw the open air. Sometimes the train went fast, sometimes it traveled slowly. And so the second day and the second night passed. We were completely exhausted. We still had some bread, but by the second day tiredness and the stench had already prevented us from getting anything more down our throats. On the third day, the train was still traveling. In the middle of the third night it stopped at a brightly lit station."*

The wagon doors were flung open. Large floodlights were directed at them, and soldiers with dogs stood on the platform. The prisoners had arrived in Auschwitz. Loudspeakers blared: *"Everyone out! Leave all luggage behind! Women to one side and men to the other!"* Otto Frank was separated from his wife and daughters. *"I shall remember the look in Margot's eyes as long as I live,"* he said later.

Nazi doctors sorted men and women into two groups. They inspected and assessed every prisoner. Rosa de Winter's turn came: *"The officer looked at me sharply. He said nothing, and merely pointed to the right. Luckily I was being sent to the good side."* Older people and mothers with small children were ordered to the other side; all of them were taken to the gas chamber right away. The gas chamber looked like a large shower room, except that the shower heads dispensed a poisonous gas instead of water. The prisoners had to undress and then get into the shower room. The door was slammed shut and before long everyone inside was dead. A special group of prisoners had to cart the corpses to the crematorium, where they were incinerated.

Like Rosa de Winter, Edith, Margot, and Anne Frank and Auguste van Pels were sent to the "good" side. They had to line up in fives and walk to the bathhouse. There they were called inside. *"We had to go to a large table,"* Rosa de Winter related. *"A girl tattooed a number on our arms with a sharp pen. I was given the number A 25250. After handing in our names, we had to undress in the presence of the SS. We were not allowed to keep anything, not even a photo. Then we were completely shaved by Polish women. SS men walked about with large dogs. We were shaking with fear, fatigue, and shame."*

Next, Rosa de Winter and the others had to take a shower. *"We were given no towels, and had to dry ourselves without. There was a draft because all the windows in the place were broken. Then we were each flung a dress, some of them thin summer dresses, others woolen dresses with long sleeves. Luckily, I was also issued a vest and a pair of underpants. There were no stockings, Shoes were handed out as well, but sometimes people got two left or two right shoes, or one with a high and one with a low heel, or clogs. By chance, I was handed a pair that fitted me fairly well. We were terribly hungry, for by now it was late in the afternoon."*

The prisoners slept in barracks: large empty barns. During the day they had to haul stones and stand about for hours in all weather while being counted. They were given very little food—a bit of cabbage soup, bread, and sometimes a little margarine.

The washbasins and the lavatories were filthy. Many prisoners fell ill, but there were no medicines. Prisoners who were too sick to work were killed in the gas chambers. Day and night, the prisoners could see the flames from the crematorium.

Trains with prisoners from various countries arrived in Auschwitz all the time. We know from Rosa de Winter that Anne burst into tears when she saw a group of Jewish children from Hungary standing waiting for half a day in the rain outside the gas chamber. Anne drew Rosa's attention to them and said, *"Just look, those eyes…"*

Otto Frank, Fritz Pfeffer, and Hermann and Peter van Pels ended up in a different part of the camp, the part reserved for men. They had to dig ditches all day, but Peter van Pels was lucky: he was given a job in the camp post office. SS men and non-Jewish prisoners were allowed parcels and letters. His work meant that Peter now and then came by some extra food, which he shared with his father, Otto Frank, and Fritz Pfeffer.

One day, Hermann van Pels bruised his thumb badly. It was to prove his death. Because he was unable to work he had to be left behind in the barracks. The Nazis inspected the barracks every day, and packed all prisoners unable to work off to the gas chamber.

Otto Frank told us what happened next. *"I shall never forget the day seventeen-year-old Peter van Pels and I saw a group of selected men in Auschwitz. Peter's father was among them. The men were marched off. Two hours later a lorry loaded with their clothes came back."* They realized that Peter's father had been murdered. After that, Otto Frank and Peter van Pels tried to keep as close to each other as possible.

In October, Fritz Pfeffer was transferred from Auschwitz to Neuengamme concentration camp near Hamburg. There he had to work even harder and received even less food. Many of the prisoners fell ill as a result and perished, Fritz Pfeffer among them. He died on December 20, 1944.

Meanwhile the German army was being driven farther and farther back by the Russians. The Nazis decided to transport all the women who could still work from Auschwitz to Germany. Nazi doctors examined them and decided which prisoners were fit for transfer. One by one the women had to step into a barracks and stand under a spotlight. Edith Frank and Rosa de Winter were assigned to the group that had to stay behind. Rosa de Winter later reported: *"Then it was the turn of the two girls, Anne and Margot. They stood there for a moment, naked and with shaven heads. Anne looked straight at us and then they were gone. We couldn't see what was happening beyond the spotlights. Mrs. Frank called out, 'The children! Oh, my God . . .'"*

After a horrific three-day journey, Anne and Margot arrived in Bergen-Belsen. Janny Brilleslijper was on the same train. Another woman described what it was like: *"We traveled for days. Every so often the train would stop because there was an air raid. After waiting for an hour, the train would continue for half an hour or so. We nearly died of hunger. When our train arrived in Bergen-Belsen we were met by SS men with bayonets fixed to their rifles. We had to leave the dead behind on the train."* The barracks in Bergen-Belsen were so full that tents were put up. Anne and Margot had to sleep in one of these. But when all the tents were blown down and broken in a storm, they were put into one of the overcrowded barracks.

Not long afterward Auguste van Pels arrived in Bergen-Belsen on a transport from Auschwitz. By then it was winter and bitterly cold, and conditions in the camp worsened by the day. The prisoners were given very little food or none at all. Infectious diseases broke out.

One evening in early December, Anne and Margot celebrated St. Nicholas's Day, Hanukkah, and Christmas all rolled together, with the other prisoners in their barracks. They sang Dutch songs and prepared a feast. Janny Brilleslijper described it as follows: *"We had saved up some stale bread and cut that into tiny pieces on which we spread onion and boiled cabbage. Our 'feast' nearly made us forget our misery for a few hours."*

In faraway Auschwitz it was even colder than in Bergen-Belsen, with a severe frost. Edith Frank had grown so weak that on January 6, 1945, she died from exhaustion.

The Russian army was slowly approaching. The Nazis were growing nervous. They wanted to evacuate the camp and destroy the evidence of their crimes. Some gas chambers and crematoria in Auschwitz were blown up with dynamite. All the prisoners who could still walk were put on transports. Otto Frank was too weak for that and had to remain in the camp. The guards planned to shoot all the remaining prisoners, but time was running out for them. They fled Auschwitz in a headlong rush because the Russians were almost at the gate. On January 27, 1945 the prisoners in Auschwitz were liberated. The Russians found a mere 7,650 people still alive. Otto Frank was one of them.

Peter van Pels was put on a transport by the Germans in the second half of January, together with the other healthy prisoners. After a dreadful journey, they arrived on January 25 at Mauthausen concentration camp, in Austria. There he was put to work in a quarry. He grew more and more exhausted and fell seriously ill in the middle of April. He died on May 5, 1945, Liberation Day in the Netherlands.

Deciding who was fit for work
and who was not on the railway
platform at Auschwitz-Birkenau

These Jewish children and the
woman with her baby are being sent
straight to the gas chamber.

Prisoners in Neuengamme camp had to work hard. They were given very little food and many died of hunger or exhaustion. Fritz Pfeffer was one of them.

Women in Bergen-
Belsen concentration
camp

Women's barracks in
Auschwitz-Birkenau

Auschwitz-Birkenau was the
largest of the extermination
camps. Estimates put the
number of people murdered
here at 1.5 million.

It often snowed in Bergen-Belsen during the first few months of 1945. Anne and Margot were freezing. Sometimes they were left without food for days on end. One day Auguste van Pels happened to run into Anne Frank's friend Hanneli Goslar. Hanneli had already been in Bergen-Belsen for a year, but in a different part of the camp. Auguste van Pels told her that Anne was there as well. Hanneli was astonished, because she had always thought that Anne had fled to Switzerland with her family. She wanted to see her right away, but that was impossible. The various parts of the camp were divided from one another by bales of straw, fences, and barbed wire.

Even so the two friends managed to talk to each other through the partition a few times. They could not see each other. The first time both of the girls cried a lot. Anne said that they had shaved her head and that she had grown very thin. She believed that her parents were dead. The next time Hanneli brought a small parcel of clothes and food for Anne and threw it over the fence. Then she heard Anne scream. *"What's happened?"* she called. Anne told her tearfully that another prisoner had grabbed the parcel. Hanneli promised to bring something else next time. She did just that, and this time the parcel reached Anne. Hanneli spoke to Anne a few more times, but after Anne was moved to another barracks at the end of February, they could no longer talk to each other.

At the beginning of February 1945, Auguste van Pels was transferred to Buchenwald camp in Germany. She died a few months later.

Margot and Anne fell ill. Janny Brilleslijper has recorded how she came across them: *"One moment Anne stood before me wrapped in a blanket. She had no tears left. Alas, none of us had had those for a long time. She said that she was crawling so much with lice and fleas that she had thrown away all her clothes. It was the depths of winter and she was wrapped in a blanket. So I collected everything I could find so that she could get dressed again."*

Margot and Anne had typhus, an infectious disease transmitted by lice. The disease starts with a high fever and a rash. Anne and Margot were lying in the barracks right next to the door. It was icy cold and there was a terrible draft. They had no warm clothes left. Time and again they called out asking to have the door shut, because they were too weak to shut it themselves. Anne and Margot died in March 1945. Janny Brilleslijper: *"First Margot fell out of bed onto the stone floor; she was no longer able to stand up. Anne died a day later."*

Anne and Margot were thrown onto a large pile of dead prisoners' bodies. A few weeks later, on April 15, 1945, Bergen-Belsen was liberated by British soldiers. As they entered the camp, they were deeply shocked by what they saw. Corpses were lying around everywhere. They had never before seen anything so terrible. Thousands of dead prisoners were buried in shallow graves and the barracks were set on fire, to prevent the spread of infectious diseases.

When Anne and Margot died in Bergen-Belsen, their father had been a free man for six weeks. He slowly regained his strength. In a letter to his mother, he wrote on March 15: *"I know nothing about Edith and the children. They have probably been deported to Germany. I long for them so much and for all of you! It is a miracle that I am still alive: I had a lot of luck and have to be grateful."*

By the end of March, Otto Frank was well enough to travel back to the Netherlands. On the way, he met Rosa de Winter. She told him that his wife had died in Auschwitz. *"Mr. Frank showed no emotion when I told him. I tried to look at him but he turned away. I think he laid his head on the table."*

British soldiers force the former camp guards in Bergen-Belsen to bury the dead.

1945 and after

The legacy

Otto Frank took a good four months to travel from Auschwitz to Amsterdam. He was forced to make a long detour because fighting was continuing in large parts of Europe. First he went to Russia and from there he took a ship to France. On June 3, 1945 he finally arrived back in Amsterdam. He was hoping and expecting that he would find his daughters Anne and Margot there.

When Otto Frank arrived in Amsterdam, he went straight to Miep and Jan Gies, who were overjoyed to see him again. But they had heard nothing of Anne and Margot. What they could tell him was that the other helpers, Bep Voskuijl, Victor Kugler, and Johannes Kleiman, had survived the war. The helpers kept wondering who had betrayed the people in hiding. They suspected Willem van Maaren, who was working in the warehouse when the group was discovered in the Annex. At the time he was already suspected of several minor thefts from the warehouse, and he had also aroused suspicion with his constant questions about the Annex. Johannes Kleiman wrote a letter to the police asking them to investigate Van Maaren. But the police were too busy with other things and did nothing.

Otto Frank tried everywhere to find out if Anne and Margot were still alive. He put an advertisement in the paper and wrote letters to all sorts of people and organizations, such as the Red Cross. He also talked to survivors returning from the camps. One day he met Janny and Lien Brilleslijper: *"Small groups kept returning from the various concentration camps, and over and over again I tried to find out if they knew anything about Margot and Anne. Finally I met two sisters who had been with them in Bergen-Belsen. They told me about the wretched last days and the death of my children."*

It was not until three days later that Otto Frank found the strength to tell the rest of his family.

Since the raid on the Secret Annex, Miep Gies had been looking after Anne's diary so that she could give it back after the war. When she learned from Otto Frank that both his daughters were dead she gave him the diary and the loose pages Anne had written, with the words: "*Here is your daughter Anne's legacy to you.*"

Otto Frank was so grief-stricken at the death of his daughters that he could not bring himself to open Anne's diary right away. It was not until weeks later that he began to read it, bit by bit. He was deeply touched by what he read and realized that he had never really known Anne. As a father he had only seen her from the outside and had no idea of all the things that were going on inside her. Later he declared: "*I started to read slowly, a few pages a day, which was all I could manage. I was flooded with painful memories. An Anne who was quite different from the daughter I had lost was appearing before me. Such deep thoughts and feelings—I had had no idea. That Anne had delved so deeply into the problem and significance of Jewish suffering through the centuries, that she had put so much energy into her faith in God, took me completely by surprise. How could I have known that the chestnut tree was so important to her, when she had never shown any interest in nature? She had kept all these feelings to herself. I also learned how important her relationship with Peter had been.*"

Otto Frank with the helpers in one of the offices at Prinsengracht shortly after the war. From left to right: Miep Gies, Johannes Kleiman, Otto Frank, Victor Kugler, and Bep Voskuijl

←

Otto Frank in the private office at Prinsengracht shows the Auschwitz tattoo on his arm.

Otto Frank with Miep and Jan Gies and their son, Paul, in 1951

Otto Frank also learned from the diary what Anne thought of her mother. "*I sometimes got very upset reading what Anne wrote about her mother. In her anger over some dispute or other she gave free rein to her feelings. It pained me to read how often Anne misjudged her mother's point of view. But it was a relief to read in later passages that Anne realized that it was sometimes her own fault that she and her mother failed to see eye to eye. She was even sorry for what she had written. Thanks to Anne's accurate description of every event and every person, all the details of our life together sprang clearly back into my mind.*"

Anne's father decided to copy some extracts from the diary for his family and friends. His friends argued that he ought to publish Anne's complete diary. At first he hesitated, but later he agreed with them. After all, Anne had written in her diary: **You've known for a long time that my greatest wish is to be a journalist, and later on, a famous writer.... In any case, after the war I'd like to publish a book called *The Secret Annex*.** (May 11, 1944)

Otto Frank tried to find a publisher, but did not succeed right away. So soon after the war, people preferred to forget all about the misery of it. Otto Frank asked Jan Romein, who was a well-known historian, to read Anne's diary. Romein was deeply impressed and wrote an article about the diary for the Dutch newspaper *Het Parool* on April 3, 1946.

"When I had finished it was nighttime, and I was astonished to find that the lights still worked, that we still had bread and tea, that I could hear no airplanes droning overhead and no pounding of army boots in the street—I had been so engrossed in my reading, so carried away back to that unreal world, now almost a year behind us."

A great many people read Jan Romein's article, and several publishers became interested and approached Otto Frank. One of them, Uitgeverij Contact, was eager to publish Anne's diary. Two years after the war, it came out under the title Anne herself had chosen: *Het Achterhuis*, or *The Secret Annex*.

The same month that the book appeared, Otto Frank talked to the police about holding an investigation into the betrayal. The letter Johannes Kleiman had written two years before was brought out from the police files and the police started the investigation. Witnesses were questioned, but that produced few results. Another problem was that many of the German police records had been blown up during a British air raid. In addition, the Nazis themselves had destroyed a lot of archive material at the end of the war. As a result, it proved impossible to find any evidence to say who had betrayed the people in the Annex. In 1948, the police decided to drop the case, but the Annex helpers continued to suspect Van Maaren.

The response to the publication of *Het Achterhuis* was so enthusiastic that the first edition was quickly sold out. Further editions followed in quick succession. Foreign publishers, too, became interested in Anne's diary. In 1950, translations appeared in Germany and France, and two years later in Great Britain and the United States, under the title *The Diary of a Young Girl*. A play based on Anne's diary was written in the United States. On October 5, 1955, *The Diary of Anne Frank* had its New York premiere on Broadway. Otto Frank did not attend this first official performance. In a letter he wrote in English to the director and to the actors, he said: *"For me this play is a part of my life, and the idea that my wife and children as well as I will be presented on the stage is a painful one to me. Therefore it is impossible for me to come and see it."*

The play was also staged in a great many other countries. A few years later, Anne Frank's diary was also made into a film. Shelley Winters, who played Auguste van Pels in the film, was awarded an Oscar for her role.

Many people who had read Anne's diary were keen to visit the Secret Annex. But that part of the building had fallen into disrepair and there were plans to demolish it. Otto Frank had not owned 263 Prinsengracht for some time. He had sold it after the war and found business premises elsewhere, where he continued to work for his company for a few years more. In 1952 he moved to Basel, where he still had family. In 1953, he married Elfriede (Fritzi) Markovits.

→

The books and papers that were the diary of Anne Frank.

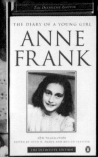

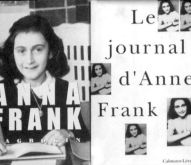

Scene from the film *The Diary of Anne Frank* with Milly Perkins as Anne Frank and Shelley Winters (right) as Auguste van Pels.

←

The Diary of a Young Girl by Anne Frank became a famous book. It was translated into more than sixty languages, and 25 million copies of it have been sold so far.

Many films and documentaries about Anne Frank have appeared over the years. In 2001 Ben Kingsley played Otto Frank in a film by Robert Dornhelm.

Anne Frank House

← Otto Frank in the attic of Anne
Frank House, a few hours before
it was officially opened in 1960.
©Arnold Newman

Some Amsterdammers felt that the Secret Annex should not be demolished. They set up the Anne Frank Stichting, a foundation that collected enough money to buy the premises. In 1960, the Annex opened to the public as a museum, the Anne Frank House. Otto Frank felt that the Anne Frank House should be more than just a museum. He wanted it to become a meeting place for young people from all over the world. The rooms in the museum were left unfurnished. In an interview, Otto Frank stated, *"During the war they took everything and I want to leave it like that."*

Because Anne's diary became so well known all over the world, more and more people kept wondering who had betrayed the people in the Secret Annex. In 1963, nineteen years after the betrayal, Karl Josef Silberbauer, the man who had led the raid on the Secret Annex, was tracked down in Austria. Silberbauer was working as a policeman in Vienna. The investigation into the betrayal was reopened and Silberbauer, the former SS man, was suspended from duty. But not even he knew who had made the telephone call to the German police that started the raid. Many witnesses had died in the meantime and the investigation yielded few results. Silberbauer was allowed to go back to work. Otto Frank did not see any reason for sending Silberbauer to prison. *"People are surprised at that. But I don't want it. For the real culprits were the men at the top. We won't get very far with punishments. What has happened cannot be undone. But we must certainly learn the lessons of the past."*

Nor did he want to point a finger at all Germans: *"I shall never forget that the Germans started this terrible war and committed all these crimes. Not just against Jews but also against the people in the occupied territories. But I do not want to generalize. There were also good Germans too, who, for instance, hid Jewish people at the risk of their own lives and who rose up against the Hitler regime. I have no prejudices at all against the younger generation."*

The identity of the traitor is still uncertain. It is possible that Van Maaren was guilty, but it may equally well have been someone else. There were quite a few others who knew that people were hiding at 263 Prinsengracht. In a busy city, it is difficult for eight people to hide for two years without any of the neighbors noticing anything. Otto Frank was reconciled to the fact that the traitor would never be found, and had this to say in 1979: *"Right now I no longer want to know who betrayed us then in Amsterdam."*

He preferred to dwell on positive issues. *"Anne's diary was a great help for me in regaining a positive outlook on the world. With its publication, I hoped to help many people in the same way, and that proved to be the case."* One year before his death in 1980, he said: *"I am now nearly ninety and my powers are slowly waning. But the duty Anne left me continues to give me new strength—to fight for reconciliation and human rights throughout the world."*

Every year thousands of people want to see with their own eyes the place where Anne wrote her diary. Unlike Otto Frank, many of the visitors do want to know who betrayed the people in hiding. In recent years, two additional names have been mentioned and given much publicity in the press. In 1998, a biography of Anne Frank was published by Melissa Müller. She had a new theory about the betrayal, alleging that there were good reasons to suspect another of the workers, Lena Hartog-van Bladeren. Lena was married to one of the men in the warehouse and worked as an office cleaner at 263 Prinsengracht. In 2002, Carol Ann Lee published a biography of Otto Frank in which she tried to prove that Tonny Ahlers, an acquaintance of Otto Frank, had been the traitor. On the basis of these new theories NIOD, the Netherlands State Institute for War Documentation, started a fresh investigation. The conclusion was that these theories, too, could not be substantiated. In all probability we will never know with any certainty who betrayed Anne Frank and the others hiding in the Secret Annex.

Some people think that all the fuss about Anne Frank and her diary is exaggerated. According to them, Anne was just one of the one and a half million Jewish children who were murdered. They believe that only when all their stories are told can we gain a real idea of what happened during the Second World War.* Primo Levi, a famous Italian writer who, like Otto Frank, survived Auschwitz, goes into this subject in one of his books: *"Perhaps it had to be,"* he wrote, *"that this one Anne Frank moves us more than all the other countless victims whose names remain unknown. If we had to share, and could share, the suffering of each one of them, we should be unable to go on living."*

Glossary

Additional information about Germany and the Netherlands during World War II.

Adolf Hitler

In 1918, Germany lost the First World War and had to pay a great deal of money to the victors, who also occupied parts of Germany. Large numbers of Germans were poor and out of work. One small political party, the NSDAP (the National Socialist German Workers' Party) promised to solve all Germany's problems. Its leader was Adolf Hitler, and his followers were called Nazis (National Socialists).

In elections, Hitler's party kept receiving more and more votes, and on January 30, 1933, Hitler was appointed Chancellor of the German Reich, the leader of the German government. The Nazis wanted a racially pure Germany. According to them, the Aryan race, to which many Germans belonged, was the best race of all. The Nazis considered other population groups to be inferior, particularly Jews, people with skin of a different color, "Gypsies" (Sinti and Roma), handicapped people, and homosexuals. All these groups, they maintained, did not belong in German society.

Anti-Semitism

Anti-Semitism is another word for hatred of Jews. Someone who hates Jews just because they are Jews is an anti-Semite. Hitler and his followers were anti-Semites. They blamed the Jews for all sorts of problems, and Jews were turned into scapegoats.

Aryan declaration

In October 1940 all Dutch civil servants and teachers had to sign an "Aryan declaration" stating whether they were Jewish or non-Jewish. After that, the Jewish civil servants and teachers were dismissed. A few months later all Jews were ordered to register as Jews. In this way, the Nazis knew precisely where to find them.

Collaboration

Some Dutch people worked with or for the German occupiers. They were known as *collaborators*. They included members of the NSB (the Dutch Nazi party). In 1941, the NSB had nearly 100,000 members. There were also some 20,000 Netherlanders who

Adolf Hitler addresses his followers in Dortmund, 1933.

German soldiers march into the ruins of Rotterdam.

served with the German army. They fought side by side with German troops against the Russians on what was called the Eastern Front.

D-day

From 1943, the Germans suffered one defeat after another. In January 1944, the Russians proved too strong for the German army at Stalingrad and the German soldiers were forced to retreat. In the west, the Allies had begun to liberate the occupied countries in Europe. On June 6, 1944, British, American, and Canadian troops landed on the beaches in Normandy in France. That day became known as D-day.

Deportations

The Nazis decided to put all Jews from Germany and the occupied territories in Europe onto trains and to "deport" them to various camps. The plan was that most of them would be murdered right away and the rest would be worked so hard that they would die of exhaustion sooner or later.

U.S. soldiers land on the beaches in Normandy in 1944.

Dictatorship

From 1933 onward, the Nazis ruled Germany with an iron fist. Germany was transformed from a democracy into a dictatorship. In a dictatorship, just one leader, the dictator, decides what is going to happen in the country. Hitler's government rounded up thousands of political opponents. They were herded into camps, where many of them were tortured and murdered.

Discrimination

The Nazis treated Jews differently from other Germans. Jews had fewer rights. The Nazis discriminated against Jews. Discrimination is the unfair treatment of a person simply because he belongs to a certain group. That group may be defined by descent, religion, or political or sexual preferences.

Dolle Dinsdag (Crazy, or Mad, Tuesday)

On September 4, 1944, the Allies liberated Antwerp. One day later the British radio claimed that Breda, too, had been liberated. Many Dutch people were beside themselves with excitement when they heard the news. In many places throughout the Netherlands, the Dutch flag was run up on September 5, or Crazy Tuesday, as it became known. Many German soldiers and members of the Dutch Nazi party fled the Netherlands. But the Allied advance was stopped. It was not until May 5, 1945, that the Netherlands was finally liberated.

Gestapo

The Geheime Staatspolizei, or Gestapo, was the name of the Nazi secret state police.

Holocaust

About six million Jews were murdered during the Second World War. This horrific event has become known as the Holocaust, or Shoah. The literal translation of the word *holocaust* is "burnt offering," *shoah* means "destruction" or "disaster."

Hunger Winter

During the winter of 1944, there was hardly any food left in the provinces of North and South Holland and Utrecht in the Netherlands, and fuel, too, was hard to find. It was a very severe winter. People felled trees, raided empty houses, and went on foot or bicycle to try and get food from farmers in the countryside. This winter became known as the Hunger Winter, and more than 20,000 people died during it.

Jewish (or yellow) star

The Nazis were determined to isolate the Dutch Jews. Their freedom was increasingly curtailed. The Jewish star was introduced in May 1942, when Jews were forced to wear a six-pointed star of David on their outer clothing. Any Jews refusing to comply were arrested and packed off to camps in Germany or Poland.

Kristallnacht

During the night of November 9, 1938, the Nazis organized a pogrom, that is, a series of violent attacks on the Jews in Germany. The Nazis laid waste to hundreds of synagogues and Jewish shops. More

Children being fed in a soup kitchen. Many children went hungry during the winter of 1944–45, particularly in the big cities.

The Yellow Star. From May 1942, all Jews above the age of six had to wear a yellow star on their outer clothing.

than two hundred Jews were murdered during this pogrom. The Nazis also arrested 30,000 Jewish men and locked them up in camps. This night came to be known as "Kristallnacht" (Crystal Night, or the Night of Broken Glass) because there was so much broken glass in the streets the following day.

NSDAP
See Adolf Hitler

Occupation of the Netherlands
On May 10, 1940, the Germans attacked the Netherlands. After a few days of heavy fighting it became obvious that the Dutch army could not win. The strength of the Germans was too great. The Dutch royal family and members of the government fled to London. On May 14, 1944, German planes blitzed the center of Rotterdam. When the German Supreme Command threatened to bomb other Dutch cities as well, the Dutch army surrendered.

Razzias, or raids
During a razzia, a street or district would be surrounded and all the houses in it searched one by one. All Jewish occupants were rounded up and put in prison. Dutch people who had hidden Jews in their homes were severely punished. From 1943 onward, Dutch men were called up for labor service in Germany. Many of them went into hiding. The Germans tried to hunt these people down as well.

Resistance in the Netherlands
At the beginning of the war many Dutch people were afraid to stand up to the Germans. Most of them tried to make the best of the new conditions. They did not assist the Germans but they did not actively oppose them, either. Later, resistance to the Germans became better organized. Resistance fighters helped people who had gone into hiding, forged documents, and published illegal newspapers. Some broke into government offices to seize food coupons and identity cards. Others freed imprisoned resistance fighters. In addition, the Dutch Resistance shot scores of Nazis and collaborators.

SWEDEN
DENMARK
GREAT BRITAIN
THE NETHERLANDS
Westerbork
Neuengamme
Amsterdam
London
Bergen-Belsen
Berlin
Warsaw
GERMANY
BELGIUM
Aachen
POLAND
Buchenwald
Normandy
Frankfurt am Main
Prague
Auschwitz
Paris
CZECH REPUBLIC
FRANCE
SLOVAKIA
Mauthausen
Vienna
Basel
SWITZERLAND
AUSTRIA
HUNGARY
ITALY
YUGOSLAVIA

Shoah

See Holocaust

World War Two, or Second World War

After overrunning the Netherlands, the German
army occupied Belgium, Luxembourg, and France.
Hitler and his generals then planned to attack Britain. The Germans also occupied many countries in
Eastern Europe. In 1941, Japanese planes attacked
American ships in Pearl Harbor (Hawaii) without
any warning, drawing the United States into war, not
only with Japan but with Germany and Italy as well.
That was because Germany had a mutual assistance
pact with Japan and Italy was an ally of Germany.
More and more countries were drawn into the war,
and it thus became a world war.

Pearl Harbor during the Japanese attack

◀ Concentration and extermination camps
mentioned in the text.

Text
Menno Metselaar and
    Ruud van der Rol
Text editor
Mariska Hammerstein
Other text and photo editors
Mieke Sobering and
    Yt Stoker
Book design
Nico de Bruijn and
    Karel Oosting
Printed in
China
Cover Design
Ed Miller
Photographs
AFS/Allard Bovenberg (142–147, 199, 200)
AFS/Collectie mw. M. Gies (99, 102, 195 ↓)
AFS/Collectie mw. R. Visser (195 ↑)
AFS/Juul Hondius (203)
AFS/Maarten van de Velde (153–157)
Arnold Newman, New York (202)
Aviodrome Luchtfotografie, Lelystad (78)
Cas Oorthuys/Nederlands Fotomuseum, Rotterdam (212 ←)
Collectie dhr. B. Elias (14)
Collectie mw. T. de Konink-ten Kley (60)
Galerie Bilderwelt Berlin (171)
Imperial War Museum, London (182, 189)
Julie Denesha (201 ↓)
Maria Austria Instituut, Amsterdam (80–91, 103, 194)
NIOD, Amsterdam (167–170, 181, 211, 215)
Panstwowe Muzeum, Oswiecim Brzezinka (183)
Twentieth Century Fox (201 ↑)
United States Holocaust Memorial Museum, Washington/
    Mark Chrzanowski (184)
Yad Vashem, Jerusalem (179, 180)

Sources
David Barnouw, Gerrold van der Stroom, *Wie verraadde
    Anne Frank?*, Uitgeverij Boom, Amsterdam, 2003
Anne Frank, *Het Achterhuis. Dagboekbrieven 12 juni 1942–
    1 augustus 1944*, Bert Bakker, Amsterdam, 2003
De Dagboeken van Anne Frank, Nederlands Instituut voor
    Oorlogsdocumentatie, Bert Bakker, 2001
Het korte leven van Anne Frank, Contact, Amsterdam, 1970
"Ich will Versöhnung", Otto Frank, *Welt am Sonntag*, 04-02-1979
"Wir sind bewusstere Juden geworden", Otto Frank, *Basler
    Magazin*, 24-02-1979
Miep Gies, Alison Leslie Gold, *Herinneringen aan Anne Frank*,
    Bert Bakker, Amsterdam, 1987
Etty Hillesum, *Letters from Westerbork*, translated by Arnold
    J. Pomerans, Pantheon Books, New York, 1986
Lin Jaldati, Eberhard Rebling, *Sag nie, du gehst den letzten Weg.
    Lebenserinnerungen 1911 bis 1988*, BdWi-Verlag,
    Marburg, 1995
Carol Ann Lee, *Anne Frank 1929–1945. Pluk de rozen en vergeet
    mij niet*, Balans, Amsterdam, 1999
Carol Ann Lee, *Het verborgen leven van Otto Frank*, Balans,
    Amsterdam, 2002
Primo Levi, *De verdronkenen en de gereddenen*, Meulenhoff,
    Amsterdam, 1986
Willy Lindwer, *De laatste zeven maanden; vrouwen in het spoor
    van Anne Frank*, Gooi en Sticht, 1988
Melissa Müller, *Anne Frank – de biografie*, Bert Bakker,
    Amsterdam, 1998
Ernst Schnabel, *Spur eines Kindes*, Fischer Taschenbuch Verlag,
    Frankfurt am Main, 1958
Jürgen Steen, Wolf von Wolzogen, *Anne aus Frankfurt*,
    Historisches Museum Frankfurt am Main, 1994
Rosa de Winter-Levy, *Aan de gaskamer ontsnapt!*, Misset,
    Doetinchem, 1945